Advance P1 Freedom Warrior

This is a fascinating and thought provoking read.

With so much noise and misinformation around about investing, wealth and financial freedom, Salena has a depth of insight that can't be denied. Her ability to communicate the complexity of investing, in parables and analogies, allows her to take people on an enriched journey to a greater understanding of wealth creation, that delivers true life freedom.

Her simple idea of being a Freedom Warrior, as opposed to investing just for the purpose of creating wealth, is both original and challenging. It's this ability to challenge that makes her such a wonderful educator.

Her highly structured models give people a blueprint for freedom, through wealth creation, and her client results are the evidence of the success of her genius and the models through which she expresses it.

Salena applies what she teaches to her own circumstances. This is real world advice from someone who is in the game everyday.

Simon Bowen
Founder The Models Method®
Creator The Genius Model®

Yes, I've read the classics on property investing and wealth creation and implemented my learnings. Those strategies have worked amazingly well for me for decades but now they no longer deliver the results I once enjoyed. The world has changed and the rules for successful property investment have to change too. The Freedom Warrior is new thinking, not a rehash of what worked a decade ago. If you want typical results do what others typically do...if you want atypical results you need an atypical plan and for me The Freedom Warrior has given me that.

Geoff Currie
CEO, Business Growth Leaders

What Salena has produced here is not just another boring property book with basic information. This is outside the box thinking, outside the box strategies and something very relevant to any property investor or business owner. Having been a property investor for over 8 years and running a business for over 9, I know the importance of having multiple wealth pillars. Salena has provided a guide to follow, how to's to use and made it easy to understand no matter what investment level you are at. Her ability to see things differently to traditional financial planners and property coaches is what makes Salena one of the best around.

Michael Griffiths
Founder, Referral Marketing Guru

For anyone serious about building wealth to create freedom in their lives then this is a must read. Salena beautifully articulates the importance of your "why" as the key factor to accelerating your financial situation. With a plethora of age-old wisdom combined with up to date insights into the current financial climate, the Freedom Warrior will give you a fresh perspective on the age-old art of wealth creation. If knowledge is power, then this book will certainly give you the power to be the freedom warrior in your life.

Brent Williams
CEO, Tomorrow Youth International

WARNING:
THIS BOOK MAY CHANGE YOUR LIFE

First published in 2018 by Salena Kulkarni
Canberra, ACT, Australia
© Salena Kulkarni

The moral rights of the author have been asserted.
This book is a SpiritCast Network Book.
National Library of Australia Cataloguing-in-Publication data:

Author:
    Kulkarni, Salena

Title:
    The Freedom Warrior; How to build a bigger life through alternative property investing strategies

ISBN-13:
    978-1-730-72826-6

Subjects:
    Wealth Creation, Property Investing, Alternative Property Investing

All rights reserved. Except as permitted under the Australian Copyright Act 1968 (for example, a fair dealing for the purposes of study, research, criticism or review), no part of this book may be reproduced, stored in a retrieval system, communicated or transmitted in any form or by any means without prior written permission. All enquiries should be made to the publisher at salena@phoenixwealthgroup.com.au

Editor-in-chief:	*Cherise Lily Nana*
Cover Design:	*Bliss Inventive*

Disclaimer:
The material in this publication is of the nature of general comment only, and does not represent professional advice. It is not intended to provide specific guidance for particular circumstances and it should not be relied on as the basis for any decision to take action or not take action on any matter which it covers. Readers should obtain professional advice where appropriate, before making any such decision. To the maximum extent permitted by law, the author and publisher disclaim all responsibility and liability to any person, arising directly or indirectly from any person taking or not taking action based on the information in this publication.

Table of Contents

PART I – BEING THE FREEDOM WARRIOR	**1**
CHAPTER 1 - THE SHIFTING SANDS OF WEALTH CREATION	3
CHAPTER 2 – AGE OLD WISDOM AND THE NEW WORLD OF PROPERTY INVESTING	17
CHAPTER 3 - THE ESSENTIAL TOOLKIT OF THE FREEDOM WARRIOR	25
CHAPTER 4 - THE SEASONS OF INVESTING	39
PART II – BLUEPRINT FOR YOUR PIPELINE	**45**
CHAPTER 5 - QUANTIFIED VISION	47
CHAPTER 6 - A SUSTAINABLE STRATEGY	59
CHAPTER 7 - ELEGANT EXECUTION	71
PART III – DEVELOP ALTERNATIVE SOURCES	**79**
CHAPTER 8 - ALTERNATIVE OPTIONS	81
CHAPTER 9 - MINDFUL DIVERSIFICATION	99
CHAPTER 10 - PROTECTED NAVIGATION	105
PART IV– BE THE CAPTAIN	**113**
CHAPTER 11 - A ROBUST RUDDER	115
CHAPTER 12 - ELEVATED MONEY WISDOM	123
CHAPTER 13 - ELITE NETWORK	133
FINAL THOUGHTS	**139**

Foreword

Creating a life of authentic freedom is the entrepreneur's dream. However, freedom isn't free. It comes with a price. It's not enough to hope for freedom. It requires intentionality. To preserve it requires a vigilant mindset and determined action.

It is not an easy goal and runs opposite to the majority of the population who too often live by default, allowing governments, other people and societal indoctrination to dictate their future.

Freedom requires a contrarian attitude. It's about following one's map, which is the road less travelled and a road that is often lonely.

The path is never without setbacks, challenges, and resets.

The Freedom Warrior, authored by my friend and colleague, Salena Kulkarni, provides the mindset and the plan that, if followed with perseverance, will guide the reader to that ultimate goal of a freedom lifestyle.

I must admit to some bias. I know Salena Kulkarni personally. It is not by accident that we met doing what we both believe is essential to a life of freedom, meeting through an international mastermind group. In this case, a tribe of like-minded entrepreneurs taking that lonely road.

It is a proven fact that going solo in life or business (or investments) is the long road filled with bumps and wrong turns. Finding people who are on the same path or have gone ahead of you in life is the fastest path to get from point A to point B. The in-between is "the gap." Moreover, it is that gap that Salena shows the reader how to close, not by working harder, but by strategically investing in international real estate properties.

This treatise is not a theoretical essay. Salena has a proven track record with a background as a chartered accountant, entrepreneur, and international investor. In *The Freedom Warrior*, she lays out the premise that a high level of active income, trading time for dollars, provides a false sense of security. Lifestyle and materialism is not a measure of true freedom. There is ultimately a day of reckoning when one either desires to stop or is forced to get off of the hamster wheel, and active income is no longer an option.

With governments around the globe accruing massive amounts of debt, it is imperative that those who want a sustainable lifestyle after active income must build net worth equity that converts to predictable lifetime cash flow. Salena has made a case for alternative investments in the real property asset class. She lays the foundation for creating a vision and reverse engineering the process with substantiated strategies vs. random investment tactics. As a global investor, she also includes a discussion of alternative investments abroad, in particular, the U.S. market, where she has considerable experience and an expansive network.

What action will you take? Will this be a book that goes on the bookshelf or becomes buried in the never-ending stack of yet-to-be-read?

Will you take a committed next step? Will you do something that you've thought about but until now has only been a dream?

What's stopping you? Your fears? Fear of what?

Freedom is not granted. It is earned. It is fought for.

It's your life. Don't live it with regrets.

Step forward now or forever hold your peace.

David Phelps, D.D.S.
Founder and CEO, Freedom Founders
Rockwall, Texas
www.FreedomFounders.com

Acknowledgements

To my best friend and darling husband Jon; thank you for inspiring and supporting me on our journey to date. Without you this book would have been a complete dud. You rock!

To my two kind, intelligent and cheeky boys; thank you for being my miracle babies. Even though you haven't really understood the whole book writing thing, I am grateful for your kind words of encouragement.

To David Phelps; for being a 'next level' mentor and giving me the support and guidance to pursue my dream of running a Mastermind. Without you, I might never have begun.

To Taki Moore; thank you for helping me get unstuck all those years ago and showing me (amongst other things) how to explain ideas in a simple effective way. Life changing stuff.

To Dave Thompson and the team at IBWR; your skilled and nurturing support has helped me achieve the unachievable. Thank you.

Dedication

In loving memory of my Dad, who gave me his all, encouraged independent thinking and taught me about perseverance and grit.

To my Mum; who brought magic to my childhood and taught me the value of nurturing relationships.

Part I

Being The Freedom Warrior

Chapter 1

The Shifting Sands of Wealth Creation

Being a property investor is no longer the pursuit of a few outliers. It is the pursuit of the masses.

Understandably, with the amount of literature and media bombarding us with messages that we 'can't rely on superannuation and the government', it's no wonder that many people are looking to property as the best alternative to filling the gap between what they want and what they might otherwise end up with.

But here's the thing.

In our pursuit of 'great properties' to invest in, we have forgotten the bigger picture of investing. Surely the purpose of investing is to create freedom. Not just lip service to a vague idea, but real, solid, definable freedom.

So what is freedom?

No doubt everyone's definition of freedom is unique. Ultimately however, financial freedom could be summed up as the ability to be free from the worry of having enough money, along with the ability to choose exactly how you want to live.

One of the things I have observed in Australia is that we try to get wealthy quietly. There seems to be social embarrassment around the idea of capitalism, because we don't want people to think that we want to be wealthy at someone else's expense. The end result of this is that we are quiet in our pursuit of wealth and freedom. In some cases we are so quiet about it that we seem apathetic, when we are certainly not.

Freedom is definitely something to be valued. It is something to be fierce about. If you aren't fierce about the pursuit of freedom, it will elude you. It's not about being loud, it's about being passionate and ferocious in the way you bring it to life. In my world, to obtain freedom, you must be a warrior.

A warrior is someone who demonstrates expanded awareness, courage, discipline, cunning, and patience. It is hard to attain financial freedom by being mild. Your ability to succeed increases exponentially when you are a freedom warrior.

> *A Freedom Warrior believes:*
>
> *They must be fierce about their pursuit of freedom. It is hard to attain financial freedom by being mild.*
>
> *They must demonstrate expanded awareness, courage, discipline, cunning, and patience.*

This book has been written specifically to challenge you on what you think you know about property investing and to have you reassess how to tackle it in order to create the freedom YOU want. Not freedom by anyone else's definition, but your own. It is to inspire you to TAKE ACTION and begin to look at the world of property investing as simply the vehicle that will get you to the freedom you want.

But here's the catch: if you don't define and aren't passionate about creating freedom, it might never arrive.

The question is, are you prepared to be fierce about your freedom?

Nobody wants to invest in property for the sake of it.

The whole point of investing is to put aside money into something that will grow in value, or provide us with income, so that sometime in the future when we want to make any life changes, we have the freedom to do so, free of worry about the financial implications.

It isn't about the money. It's about the freedom that comes from having the choice to spend your time exactly as you choose. Time is your most precious commodity. No matter how wealthy you are, you're never going to get back even a nanosecond of your yesterdays.

Money is the most powerful way to take back your time.

If you could stop trading your time for money (where the money seems to go out as fast as it comes in), what would that mean to you?

Sadly, although it's widely recognised that property investing is the most accessible and lucrative form of investing, it comes at a time when getting results from property investing has never been harder.

Statistics tell us that nearly 8% of the Australian population are property investors (I'd hazard a guess that at least another 5% want to be property investors). Of that 8%, only 0.065% actually go on to own five or more properties. What does this tell us?

Some people 'wing it' and might do ok. But most people who want to create wealth from property flounder.

I speak to countless property investors each year who are struggling to get results. Who are disheartened by their efforts with property investing. Who feel that they can't get a break. Who are flustered and fear that they won't have the money they need in retirement.

As a keen student of what is happening in the world of property investing, one thing is apparent. Taking the actions that have worked in the past will no longer get you the same results as in years gone by.

> *A Freedom Warrior understands:*
>
> *Money is the most powerful way to take back your time.*

The time has come to stop, take stock and try something else.

But here are the challenges:

First off, the marketplace is significantly more crowded than it was even ten years ago. Over the last two generations, we have seen the ability to secure great opportunities in property go from 'plentiful' to 'scarce'. An intention to make money in property investing and a theoretical understanding of what's possible just isn't enough anymore. Ultimately this means is that it's getting tough to find lucrative property deals in a marketplace already filled with hungry property investors.

Secondly, the market is flooded with information which may or may not be helpful to you and your investing journey. There is an abundance of educators, advisers, marketers, bankers, and media sources all vying for your attention. For newbie investors this makes it overwhelming to sift through the noise and decide what is real. The property sales industry has evolved into a marketplace where it is difficult to gauge what is important and what isn't. Each player desperately trying to tell/sell you that their perspective is the right one. Common sense is often lost behind skewed facts & statistics, all designed to compel you to take action.

> *A Freedom Warrior recognises:*
>
> *Not many people who give advice about money and wealth are rich because they have been great investors themselves. They are rich because their business pays them handsomely.*

And finally, the market has become unbelievably expensive. It's no longer a small gamble to take a punt on a property. As the average price of property has skyrocketed well past $500k (half a million dollars?!!), investors have to be more discerning about what they strive to buy. Adding even one or two 'lemons' to your portfolio of investment properties can be crippling because of the scale and volume of resources required for each investment.

In summary, property is harder to transact, margins have become skinnier, and economics are more uncertain and complex.

All these things provide friction. Their impacts can range from simply slowing us down a little, to creating insurmountable obstacles. What we are all really worried about is that time is running out. Have we done enough to create the kind of financial future and legacy that we thought we would?

But now here's the good news:

If you get it right, you can begin to identify opportunities that others are overlooking and from which you can cherry-pick as and when you decide.

You can develop the right filters so that it becomes apparent which voices are congruent with your plan and which are not. If you get it right, your ability to find and attract those people to support your property investing journey is simplified and your skills as a property investor can be amplified.

The need to build a massive asset base is diminished. The focus is on effective property investing rather than volume. You can begin to focus on the minimum effective investments needed to achieve the financial freedom you want. You can discern between opportunities that are 'a fit' for you, versus those that will be more speculative, or a distraction.

This is what has led me to start challenging 'conventional wisdom' when it comes to property investing. It is 100% true that over history there are people who have managed to create wealth in literally any market conditions. Who were these people? What did they do differently?

Instead of doing what others are doing, what if I got really clear about who I am and what I want, worked out how to find opportunities that others weren't thinking about, but above all else, found out how to build my network in a way that generated opportunities as I needed them?

Who is this book for?

This book is for business owners and executives who want to understand a framework that can be adapted to work in any environment or market conditions. This book is for people who recognise that although business and high-paying corporate roles can be lucrative, they aren't the path to freedom.

For many people, being in business is a cash-cow. For some executives, it might seem that the gravy train will never end. The reality, though, is that fortunes can change in a heartbeat... an unexpected event, economic change, government intervention...and so on.

Most of the smartest business people of all time take their hard-earned business income and switch it into more stable assets like property. This is how they 10x their wealth. It's not from selling their business.

Executives do the same. They deploy as much of their income into income-producing capital assets so that when they say 'goodbye' to the workplace, the cash just keeps rolling in.

> *A Freedom Warrior understands:*
>
> *Most of the smartest business people of all time, take their hard-earned business income and switch it into more stable assets like property. This is how they 10x their wealth. It's not from selling their business.*

If I were to articulate the needs of a successful property investor, I would say there are a few vital ingredients:

1. You need a system to fast-track your knowledge and understanding of property so that you can implement fast and avoid pitfalls.

2. You need a framework to help you access and deploy your hard-earned money and disposable income to maximise the return you achieve.
3. You need a plan to replace all or a large part of your income, so that at some defined point in the future you can make the choice to work or not work.
4. You need access to people you trust who can guide you when you need it and give you an inside track to opportunities ahead of the masses.

For me, it has never been about trying to earn more money through my business. The game has been, 'how can I take the income that I earn and translate it into income-generating assets that gradually replace my entire living expenses?' I love teaching people how to create financial freedom. I believe it is part of my calling in life.

The pressure to succeed in modern day society is higher than ever. We are busy beyond what sometimes seems reasonable and much of our daily lives is spent juggling work, family and personal commitments. Time is precious and scarce. Investing is something that falls into the category of important, but not urgent.

While most busy professionals and business owners like the idea of creating wealth, driving it forward mindfully often just seems like more hard work in an already busy life.

This books takes you through the key ideas and frameworks you need to set yourself apart as a property investor and how to deploy your hard-earned capital carefully and effectively to fast-track your path to the sort of freedom that is meaningful to you.

As we move towards an economy when change is implemented at the speed of thought, doing business seems to be getting harder and slightly more confusing.

I take my hat off to those people in business who are really kicking big goals. I have had fantasies in my past of being a Richard Branson type, but recognise now that is simply not my genius.

What my genius is however, is working with people who recognise that while their business or employer might be their cash-cow, the smartest exit strategy of all is to be thinking about how to build an alternative pillar of wealth through property investing.

Selling a business for a lump sum of cash that you plan to use as your nest egg can be tough for many businesses, so it's super important to be thinking in terms of how to develop a secondary stream of cash-flow while you have the means to do it.

> *A Freedom Warrior knows:*
>
> *The smartest exit strategy of all is to be thinking about how to build an alternative pillar of wealth through property investing.*

For the executive, the superannuation you've been diligently squirrelling away is honestly going to have to be pretty 'meaty' by the time you hit retirement to be impactful.

This isn't about trying to step out of your business or work because you don't love what you do, it's about creating choice.

Before you charge forward, I want to share some ideas with you that will explain the 'lay of the land'. To skip ahead would otherwise be like jumping out of a plane and missing the safety briefing.

The Great Wealth GAP

The story is a familiar one. A smart person attracted to the idea of wealth, but with little time put towards their financial matters.

The wealth gap is not a reference to some gap between rich and poor. It is a reference to the unforeseen GAP that most successful people don't anticipate as their lives unfold. It is the GAP between the image people hold of what life beyond work looks like and what they can actually afford.

What is incredible, is the number of people who earn a fabulous living and assume that minimal attention to their future investments will still get them over the line.

It's very easy when you are a high income earner to have all of the lifestyle and accessories that go along with that. Certainly to the outside world you can project great success around money.

The reality for the majority of people though, is that if their income stream were to dry up tomorrow, all of that wealth or 'perceived wealth' would evaporate.

Financial freedom isn't the same as being rich. Although people often confuse the two, they are completely separate goals. One person could be completely financially free, earning $30,000 per year. Another person could be trapped, even with millions of dollars.

The scary part about the wealth GAP is that so few people give it any attention.

> *A Freedom Warrior understands:*
>
> *High income and high net wealth are not the same thing....*
>
> *...and never, ever judge a person by the car they drive.*

When most people are in their prime earning years, it is easy to throw attention toward wealth and wealth management on the back burner.

But here's the kicker: if we think about the range of possible financial futures we might have, ranging from epic to diabolically bad, the longer we give ourselves to change our trajectory, the easier it is to change gears and get a good result.

In other words, if the runway to retirement is short, the ability to change track is in many cases irrecoverable. It is really important, regardless of where you are on the runway to retirement, that you stop, reflect and decide if now is the time to give it some attention.

But only you can drive the change. Nobody else. Nobody cares about your money as much as you do.

> *A Freedom Warrior believes:*
>
> *Nobody cares about your money as much as you do.*

Australia's Love Affair With Property Investing

Australia has evolved into a nation of people who love property and property investing. It's not hard to understand why; there are countless stories of people becoming multi-millionaires by riding the wave of success with their property investing.

People on modest incomes have scrounged and saved their deposits for properties and have been able to use the growth in the property values to drive their ongoing investing and massive equity gains.

We have magazines, media reports and websites all dedicated to fuelling our love of property investing.

So let's examine the good, the bad and the ugly.

Firstly, it is indeed possible to make a passive income stream from property. The sad news is that as property prices continue to rise sharply, the metrics push everything out of whack and it is getting pretty tough to develop much income within the first few years of holding an Australian property.

Imagine you are in the market for a typical residential investment property. The median house price in Australia is now soaring past half a million (and some sources claim as high as $800k). That's a lot of money by anyone's standards. Now imagine you hold that property with no debt… initially this might seem exciting, right? But if we assume a super-exciting yield of say 5% (the Australian average is reported as 3.83%), you might say this equates to a modest income. Then deduct the typical holding costs such as rates, insurances, property management, possible vacancy and maintenance. Let's say this equates to between 2-3% of the property value. Suddenly your income stream drops to between 1-3%.

Now I don't know about you, but I personally think that's a pretty crappy return. If you had a million dollars invested, would you be excited by an income stream of $10,000 to $30,000?

Secondly, the number of people actually achieving any degree of success with their investing results is dwindling.

I mentioned earlier that an estimated 0.065% of our population actually make it to owning five or more properties. This means that about one in every one hundred investors is actually having any sizeable degree of success.

Imagine that one in one hundred!

A Freedom Warrior accepts:

> *The Australian model for average residential property investing is flawed. It's great for building capital, but when you need an income stream, it doesn't deliver much.*

This book is not only about how to position yourself to be that one in one hundred, but how to do it in a way that has never been tackled before.

Albert Einstein's View On Change

One of the biggest challenges for property investors today is that people are looking for the shortcut to wealth. In particular, we are hungry to see what everyone else is doing to guide our own investing decisions. That's how millions of dollars-worth of 'get rich quick' courses have been sold from the stage.

Surely this is a reasonable approach?

Perhaps. But, in a marketplace which is now crowded, where information is everywhere and where people are time-poor and want to get results asap, doing what others are doing is not necessarily going to get you the results you want.

Paul Rulkens did a TED talk where the idea he wanted to share was that the majority is always wrong and that only 3% of people look beyond what everyone else is doing.

He tells the story of how in 1942, Albert Einstein was teaching at Oxford University. It was reported that he gave his senior physics students exactly the same exam he had given them the year before. His assistant assumed it to be a mistake, but Einstein confirmed that the exam was exactly the same. The assistant thought Einstein was 'losing it', but Einstein is quoted as replying, "...the questions are still the same, but the answers have changed."

Many people have gone on to show that this same principle applies in the world of finance and economics. In other words, doing what everyone else is doing isn't going to get you the amazing outcome it once did.

The majority of investors just keep doing what they know over and over again. We go through sixteen years of schooling where the main premise is that history is the best teacher and then step into life expecting that if we replicate what others have done in the past, we will achieve the same results or better.

Perhaps this even works some of the time.

> *A Freedom Warrior recognises:*
>
> *For success as an investor, you need to tread a different path to the majority.*

The issue is that we aren't taught to take into consideration new things and things that could happen, but have never happened before. The majority keep doing what worked in the past and expect the same result. What's more, when they're not happy with the result, an individual, institution or country starts to do more of the same, expecting better results.

Investors who follow the herd invariably end up buying at or near the top of booms when the media and the so-called 'experts' are most euphoric. Then they often sell when everybody else is selling, when the media is most pessimistic at the bottom of the busts.

And so… our goal as a freedom warrior is to step outside of conventional wisdom and find ways to collectively 'next level' our investing results.

Chapter 2

Age Old Wisdom and the New World of Property Investing

A Bucket Carrying World

I have always loved parables as a way to impart wisdom.

Many investors have been inspired to think about investing because they've heard or read about some version of 'the parable of the pipeline'.

This story is simple and yet it has been responsible for inspiring thousands of people to try their hand at becoming investors.

I have heard a bunch of versions told of this story over the years, some more elaborate than others, but in a nutshell, the gist of it is as follows:

One thousand years ago, two friends lived in a village near a large lake. They both decided to set up businesses that would deliver water to the village.

The first friend used his strength and stamina to carry bucket after bucket to the village. The villagers were overjoyed and paid him handsomely for his efforts. As long as he showed up to work and carried the buckets, he kept getting paid.

The other friend started similarly, by carrying the water, but eventually recognised that his body was wearing out and that whenever he stopped, the income stopped as well. He was inspired to take a different approach and decided to design and build a pipeline.

He worked really hard... I mean really hard, to build the pipeline on his own. He was mocked and ridiculed by the villagers for his ideas, but eventually the pipeline was completed and the village was able to benefit from the water that flowed directly from the lake to the village with the simple turn of a tap.

He became the town hero.

He started to collect money day and night and barely had to lift a finger. His friend eventually went out of business, but was later invited to join forces with him and together they developed multiple pipelines.

They both retired young and with great freedom to use their resources as they chose. They attempted to share this wisdom with others, but many preferred the 'old school' and understood method of carrying the buckets.

Fast forward one thousand years and we see that not much has changed.

As mentioned, I often witness confusion in investors between high income and high net wealth. In other words, most of us confuse bucket carrying for pipeline building. Essentially a job of any variety, including most businesses, is a modern-day version of bucket carrying.

Since the idea of high income is held up as the ideal, it is not surprising that most people believe that the pathway to success is to find a job or business that pays well.

> *A Freedom Warrior comprehends:*
>
> *Most of us confuse bucket carrying for pipeline building.*

Having worked with many 'high income' earners over the years though, I can tell you now that regardless of their income, most are only a few pays from broke. In other words, if the business or other paid income stopped tomorrow, the ticking clock to bankruptcy would be a matter of months.

Here is the way we are told to be successful in life:

- We are told by our parents that the way to succeed in life is to find the biggest possible bucket.
- Go to school and figure out a way to get a bucket.
- As you get into the workforce, try to grow the size of your bucket.
- As you get older and you create a family and other responsibilities, work even harder to upgrade your bucket to cope.

- Pray the bucket is big enough to carry you through retirement.
- Fantasise about what you will do when you can hang up your bucket.

The majority of bucket carriers will put an enormous amount of energy into growing the bucket, or in some cases trying to carry multiple buckets. More buckets means more income, right?

Whether you are in business, or you work for someone else, if you sell your time for money, then you are effectively carrying a bucket.

The good news is that in our modern world, there is a growing awareness that investing and building a pipeline of passive income could be the way to putting our bucket down sooner. However, as it's unfamiliar and fraught with perceived dangers, it gets tossed into the 'too hard bucket'... (hahaha!). It seems simpler to just keep working and doing what's familiar, than to learn or think about a different path.

The lesson? No matter how big your bucket is, when you stop, it stops being filled.

This book endeavours to show you the path to true freedom and why, if you aren't fierce about building your pipeline, you will remain trapped in the bucket-carrying mode.

The principle of effective investing is to work hard to develop your first pipeline and then leverage that effort. The choice we all face is whether to stop putting all our efforts into bucket carrying and start to divert some of our precious time and money into building a pipeline. In other words, pay a little bit now, to create freedom sooner at a significantly more amplified rate. The alternative is a big cost later, when you might be working years beyond when you might have liked, or your savings bucket falls short.

Some may laugh at us. Some may even shame us for this pursuit.

In my own experience, I have often felt judged by those who thought I should have taken a more conventional path as a Chartered Accountant. Luckily for me, a niggling feeling that building a pipeline was infinitely more fun and would create more freedom over the long-term, propelled me into this space.

High income and high net wealth are not the same thing. Too many people confuse these ideas. More money from working can often appear to be a step towards being 'richer', but if your bigger bucket is going towards more lifestyle spending, it's really just creating the 'illusion' of wealth.

If wealth is about building a pipeline, or in other words, a self-sustaining income stream, perhaps it could even be measured by how long you could afford to not work. Becoming wealthy has little to do with luck, intelligence or education. Becoming wealthy requires patience, self-discipline, determination and effort. Sometimes it can require a compromise in lifestyle, figuring out how much you are prepared to go without now, to reap the benefits of your pipeline in the future.

The extension of being wealthy can be freedom, but not always. Plenty of wealthy people still work themselves to the bone, feel financial pressure and have little time.

Why?

Because true freedom requires awareness and a framework that guides actions.

The Point?

Although this parable is a story that has been told and retold many times, the extension I want to add, is that knowing you need to build a pipeline just isn't enough anymore. It takes more skill, awareness and agility than in years gone by.

> *A Freedom Warrior understands:*
>
> *Knowing you need to build a pipeline just isn't enough anymore.*

Sliding Doors

Do you remember the movie 'Sliding Doors'?

Sliding Doors was a fun romantic comedy in the nineties about how there are forks at every point in the road that can lead us to completely different outcomes. Real life is also a continuous series of 'sliding doors' that can lead us to completely different outcomes.

If you reflect on where you are now in your life financially, and imagine where you might like to be in say 10-15 years, you may consider a few possible outcomes:

1. Firstly, you might imagine a future that looks super bright. Where time and money are plentiful and you are well above average wealth standards. You have maximised the premium income you have had over time by building beautiful pipelines that bring you income. You work from time to time because you like to, but in general you enjoy your time following your passions.
2. You might also imagine a future that looks a little less bright, where perhaps you are moderately comfortable and slightly above average in your wealth position. You have tried to put aside energy towards building your pipeline, but on the whole, you have minimised your effort and taken the conventional path. Your primary focus over time has been on growing your bucket. Unfortunately, you have been unable to reduce the pressure of your workload and the idea of an early retirement seems unlikely.

3. Imagine a future where things are a bit skinny. You can make ends meet, but you have had to let go of most of the luxuries you had hoped to enjoy. There had been little emphasis on building any kind of pipeline, but it feels too late now to roll up your sleeves and start now. When you think of retirement, it seems to still be some way off. It's not ideal, but you recognise you need to soldier on.
4. Things are in a really depressing state. You are looking down the barrel of a shortfall in lifestyle when you stop working. You anticipate working at a time when others have long since retired. Your family might be thinking about how they might have to support you in the future.

Which of these scenarios seems most likely to you right now?

Which one would you like it to be?

The good news is that the jump from one possible future to another is a small tweak to the 'doors' you slide open right now. It's about committing the time and resources to building your pipeline now.

The longer you postpone the decision to take a different path, the harder it is to make an impactful change. The really sad news is, that if you leave the decision to open a different door till too late into the future, your ability to recover financially is almost impossible.

And here's the bonus. If you are already on pathway number one, then the model I am about to unveil will simply shorten the timeline and bring forward the freedom closer to today.

The New World Of Property Investing

As powerful and as widely understood as the fable of the pipeline story is, there is mass confusion in the market about how to succeed as a pipeline builder.

While the schooling systems don't really teach us much about wealth, there are still plenty of people and sources of information out there telling us to go out there and 'just build our passive income'. Truthfully though, this is a tough call. In a competitive marketplace, where there is an avalanche of information available, the question becomes, 'but which path should I take?'

More and more people understand the need to develop a pipeline, but not many people know how.

After years of working with hundreds of budding investors, the framework that follows represents the essential ingredients property investors need in order to build the pipeline of their dreams.

Chapter 3

The Essential Toolkit of the Freedom Warrior

S o let's start at the beginning.

First of all, it can sometimes be hard to articulate our motivations for creating wealth. The simplest word to capture the common theme that I hear people express, is freedom. What most people are striving for at an unconscious level is some flavour or variety of freedom.

THE FREEDOM WARRIOR FRAMEWORK™

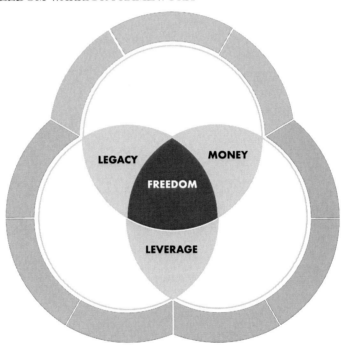

I am passionate about helping people use property investing as the pathway to achieve total freedom. It is important to emphasise again here that property investing is simply the tool to achieve the outcome we want.

What I mean by this specifically, is freedom on three levels. Freedom with money, freedom to leverage time and resources, and the freedom to create an enduring legacy.

1. Money

    Money is about flow. The major limitation that people experience around flow is that they are carrying buckets.

    If we were to articulate what it is that most people are striving for, it is high continuous flow, as distinct from carrying buckets.

    Regardless of income level, money seems to create stress and limitations in people's lives.

    Imagine this. A student doctor fantasies about how their life will be different when they are earning a high income as a fully qualified surgeon. But as time passes, they continue to enjoy bigger lifestyle expenses with every incremental increase in income. They've earnt it. They've worked hard. They deserve it. Years after becoming a well-known reputable surgeon and earning in excess of a million dollars a year, the money tension has not shifted. They still feel money strain and now pressure to continue earning to support new responsibilities.

    While not always the case, it is true that for the majority, as your income grows, your desire to indulge in more lifestyle expenditure also increases. Hence the idea that increasing your income will bring you financial freedom is not necessarily true.

    Now imagine a situation where money flowed into your bank accounts and covered your living expenses regardless of whether you worked or not. The way you live your life, the possibilities and self-imposed limits might change considerably.

The flow of money is one dimension of freedom that can have a transformative impact on our lives.

2. Leverage

This is about your ability to multiply your efforts to create more time and resources.

Consider the use of a fulcrum. The effect of a fulcrum in the context of lifting heavy objects, is that it makes lifting something that is impossible, possible.

It is commonly said, that it isn't how much you earn, but what you do with it, that has the greatest impact on your wealth over time. The main prize of earning higher income and carrying a larger bucket, is that it gifts us with the capacity to take action and use that income to create wealth more rapidly.

The beauty of leverage is that it reduces the efforts we need to dedicate towards achieving our goals. It means we can achieve goals quickly, so that our time and resources are put to best use.

If you have no leverage, your ability to multiply your results is massively diminished.

3. Legacy

At a certain time in your life, you stop worrying about yourself and start worrying about others, whether it is friends, family, our tribe, causes or community.

Legacy is often the unspoken and more subtle element of financial freedom. We all want to feel like we've made a contribution beyond just that of filling our own cup. And yet, to powerfully enable legacy requires an ability to freely dedicate time, resources and money.

It should be the case that as wealth is passed down to the next generation, that the family tribe becomes increasingly wealthier. That is certainly far from the reality of most Australians. More often than not, parents spend their wealth (or the bulk of it), leaving their kids in a position where they must start wealth building again.

Legacy is the freedom to dedicate and share wealth with others, whether it's your time, resources or money.

For me, the motivation to achieve these things in my life has always been crystal clear.

When I was ten years old, my parents shared with me that my dad had been diagnosed with a terminal illness. It was my mum that shared the news with me and at the time, the prognosis was that he might have a window of perhaps six months.

Needless to say, as a young child, I was really rocked.

Fortunately for all of us, during that window of time, a new technology was developed that gave my dad a small extension on life. The technology was new however, and no one understood how effective it would be, or how long it would give him. They estimated another six months.

At the end of that six months, they again told him that he might have another twelve months... and so it went, on and on, maybe another twelve months... in fact he went on to live another thirty years and when his time was up, he left on his own terms.

Sadly, my dad never really shared any of that with me till the last two weeks of his life.

What I witnessed was a man whose switch was flicked overnight. He went from a happy-go-lucky sort of guy, to a man whose only concern was how his wife and two daughters might survive without him. I couldn't understand it at the time, but I often felt his pain around money; the worry and his burning desire to see my sister and I become independent, successful women.

My dad busted his butt to give us everything he could. He was generous with us to a fault and he shouldered the burden of his health like a quiet soldier. His treatment was painful and stressful, but he rarely complained about it.

Watching his journey taught me many things.

Firstly, I am 100% clear that you never know when your time is up. We all behave as if we have forever to live - that we can postpone important things till tomorrow. I try hard not to do this.

Secondly, my dad's relationship with money had a profound influence on me. I decided I didn't ever want to have the sort of money worries that I had witnessed in my dad. I wanted to have a good relationship with money. I wanted the freedoms that come with having my own pipeline. I wanted to build something robust that could weather any storm. I absolutely want the freedom to be with my family as I choose and to create a legacy beyond my own existence.

As with our fable, we can either be the bucket carrier or the person who builds a pipeline. To achieve more money flow, to amplify your efforts, time and resources and to give you the ability to create a bold legacy, you need to focus on three big things:

THE FREEDOM WARRIOR FRAMEWORK™

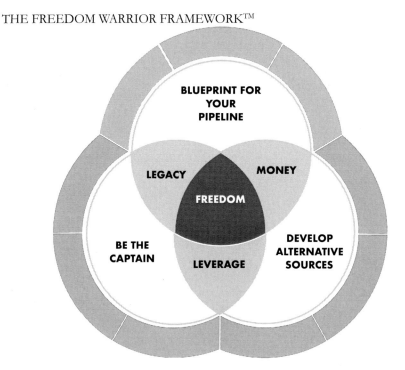

1. Blueprint For Your Pipeline

Imagine a garden hose trying to fill a dam. The trickle is there, but it is slow. If you are not in a hurry, this might be tolerable. For those with places to go and things to do, this idea of a more substantial pipe that will fill the dam quickly is of greater appeal.

Imagine you want to fill your dam not over the course of your life, but well before retirement age. You need the design and the apparatus to build something big that can carry significant amounts of water.

This element really forms the foundation for the whole model and it is important that in looking at new opportunities that this becomes the filter through which these opportunities are assessed.

This is all about planning BIG.

Without a blueprint for your pipeline, you have no direction.

2. Develop Alternative Sources

As the developer and owner of your pipeline, it is vital that you examine where you are drawing your water from. Are you drawing your water from multiple sources?

The river nearby can ebb and flow with the seasons. At times it can flow with strength and at other times it can dry down to a trickle. If this is the only resource your pipeline relies on, then at times it will run well and at other times you will have to patiently wait for a change in season to continue your ability to develop opportunities.

But... if you were to walk over the hill and up into the mountain range, you might find there is a huge lake up there, with another river going past. If you made the effort to find out and understand these alternate water sources, you could tap into those as well. This would not only increase your capacity but would mitigate against changing conditions.

This becomes an issue of water security. In a similar way that many governments try to draw water from multiple sources, it is necessary to ensure that the pipeline can maintain sufficient flow along with diversifying the risk of reliance on one source.

This is all about playing BIG.

Without developing alternative sources, you have no ability to adapt to changing market conditions.

3. Be The Captain

Once your pipeline is established and the water needed for your own uses is satisfied, the mind can turn towards ideas of helping others. Perhaps your tribe, village or even the rest of the world can benefit from the pipeline you have created.

It is necessary to elevate your thinking.

The journey becomes one of examining the ways to improve the strength and capacity of your pipeline. What are the best materials, what is the best way to build to endure for a long time, and who are the experts that you need to support ongoing flow?

Building an enduring pipeline is about developing your thinking, surrounding yourself with people who understand best practice. If you use the wrong materials or the wrong people, you are going to build a pipeline that breaks down.

You start to consider whether the pipeline will give you not only the capacity that you want, but also the longevity.

Capacity is about making sure you have enough to take care of the needs beyond your own.

Longevity is about considering how to set up your pipeline so that it lasts.

These require patience and perseverance to put in place measures that allow the pipeline to endure beyond your existence and attention.

Also consider that being the Captain is a recognition that creating substantial wealth is like guiding a large ship. Without a captain coordinating effort, the ship can easily get off course, run into obstacles or in the worst-case scenario, sink. To successfully guide a ship, the captain needs wisdom to judge and adapt to conditions, relationships with great people to crew the ship for them and a ship with a sensitive steering system to move in the desired direction.

This is all about thinking BIG.

Without becoming the Captain, you have no ability to endure.

> *A Freedom Warrior knows:*
>
> *If you have a blueprint for your pipeline (you PLAN BIG) and you become the Captain (you THINK BIG), then you have LEGACY.*
>
> *If you have a blueprint for your pipeline (you PLAN BIG) and you develop alternative sources (you PLAY BIG), then you have MONEY.*
>
> *If you become the Captain (you THINK BIG) and you develop alternative sources (you PLAY BIG), then you have LEVERAGE.*

Let's go deeper into this framework.

To be The Freedom Warrior and master wealth and property investing, you need to know how to accelerate your progress.

Within each of the three big elements, there are nine projects that must be implemented to accelerate our results.

The three keys projects to building the blueprint for our pipeline are:

1. Develop a quantifiable vision - This is about defining what we want, what success looks like and having clarity on where we are right now. Without this, we lack direction.
2. Create a sustainable strategy - This is about building the blueprint that will drive our investing actions. We want to make sure we invest in opportunities that fit our means, risk appetite, our major life milestones and marry up with our need and wants.
3. Prepare for elegant execution - This is all about putting in place the components of our investing engine that enable us to smoothly transact as and when we need to. As opportunities present themselves, we need to have a framework to prepare a business case, harness a team to execute and skillfully distill opportunities to extract only the best ones.

The three key projects to developing alternative sources requires us to:

1. Create an awareness of alternative investment options - This is about becoming familiar with opportunities that might otherwise be considered beyond our reach or comfort zone and recognising that there are ways to incorporate these into our plan in a safe and methodical way.
2. Develop mindful diversification - This is about bringing a higher level of awareness to the way in which we implement diversification in our investing. Instead of giving 'lip service' to this idea, it is about bringing a more structured approach to the way we accumulate investments.
3. Operate a navigation system that keeps us protected - It is critical when trying new and exciting investment opportunities that we remain safe. Staying protected is about developing the systems and frameworks to filter opportunities and reduce risk.

The three key projects which give us the strength to be the Captain are:

1. Our ability to play the long game - An important aspect of wealth creation for many people is how to share that wealth with

others beyond our own lives. It is the development of ideas and structures that can be used to bring those people and causes that we love, into alignment with our intentions and hopes for the use of the wealth we intend to pay forward. We might liken this to the rudder of a ship. It is important for a large vessel to have a robust rudder.

2. Capacity to develop elevated money wisdom - This is an essential part of becoming the Captain. It is the development of the way we think and act around money. Growing wealth to the next level requires high awareness and an ability to be a stellar steward of our capital.

3. The strength of our elite network - For many, this is the single most important element of wealth creation. Without this piece, the best laid plans can become useless. Our network is the primary driver of our success, so it is critical we cultivate it in all the right ways.

THE FREEDOM WARRIOR FRAMEWORK™

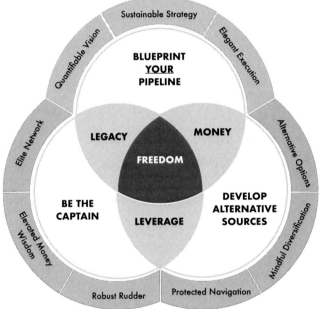

Each of these nine projects forms a building block that all professional investors rely on. I would encourage you to assess your strength against each of these elements as being at one of three possible levels:

RED - I haven't addressed this at all, or don't know anything about it.
AMBER - I have some ideas, but need some work here.
GREEN - I am all over it!

It is important to feel confident about all of these in order to build the full armour of the Freedom Warrior!

An investor isn't a professional investor because they spend more time looking for things to invest in. A professional investor is one who understands the importance of preparation and makes sure all elements of strength and weakness have been considered and accounted for.

> *A Freedom Warrior is aware that:*
>
> *A professional investor is one who understands the importance of preparation and makes sure all elements of strength and weakness have been considered and accounted for.*

This book is intended to open up dialogue designed to put you firmly on the path of becoming a professional investor.

The freedom warrior is really the person who has the ability to **LIVE BIG.**

Chapter 4

The Seasons of Investing

'Not all investors should be lumped into a single bucket'.

As our wisdom around creating wealth evolves, it is important to recognise that so too does our awareness as an investor. At each stage of our evolution, we need different things, have different aspirations and need different people to support our journey.

The simplest metaphor to understand these transitions is to talk about the seasons. An ability to understand which season you are in, is what will drive which aspect of the Freedom Warrior Framework™ you should be most focused on.

First and foremost, it is important to mention that a person's income level doesn't necessarily relate to the season they are in. The season is a reflection of important habits, priorities and actions that are driving your wealth.

THE FREEDOM WARRIOR SEASONS™

The typical journey of a property investor looks something like this:

SPRING - BUILDING SURPLUS

This is the season to harness your resources and cultivate good money habits.

When you first enter the workforce, or when property investing as a concept gets on your radar, what you want to do is work as hard as you possibly can to accumulate surplus cash so that you can kick off your property investing journey.

This is really a pre-investor stage. Although you may not hold many (or any) assets at this time, it is your opportunity to educate yourself, design and prepare for the future. In our current world there is no doubt that this is a tough challenge. Life is expensive and filled with distractions and subtle signals to focus on spending in the now.

Your level of passion and determination in the initial stages will set the foundations and determine your ability to quickly progress your journey as an investor.

SUMMER - TRACTION

This is a season where you need strong returns to give you traction.

At the beginning of your journey as an investor, you want your money to work as hard for you as possible. The goal in the early days when you are investing is to amass as much of a capital base as you can, be aggressive and accelerate as quickly as you can. You want your money to do as much heavy lifting as possible, mostly in terms of capital growth, because additional cash-flow isn't as important to you while you are working.

As you build your asset base, you find yourself constantly looking for ways to tweak and grow it. This season is all about wanting to maximise your capital base.

My experience working with many investors tells me that this is where most people get stuck, or stop. An investor may have done a good job to build their asset base, but then find themselves hitting a plateau. It can occur for many reasons, but most commonly, the banks don't want to lend any more money, or lifestyle expenses increase, putting further investing on ice.

Most investors don't probe any further and hope that the assets they have in place will perform over time.

AUTUMN - OPTIMISING

This is where you work with the assets you have to optimise them and bridge the last part of the gap between where you are and where you want to be before retirement (or achieving freedom).

For those few investors that push into this season, this is the place where you start asking the question 'what else'.

The emphasis now is on just beginning to turn the dial away from trying to build more capital and more towards generating an income stream on your capital base. Again, this is where many property investors struggle and may tolerate poor income streams simply because they don't know 'what else' to do.

This season is about making the most of what you have and trying to make sure you hold the optimal blend of assets. Access to the right education and resources, but above all else, the right people, will determine how easily you transcend this stage.

WINTER - PRESERVING

And finally Winter. This is the season where you say, 'I am in preservation mode'.

As you reach your ideal capital base, the emphasis changes. You may no longer have an interest in making your capital work as hard for you as possible, but more want to focus on protecting it and having it generate a healthy, but not necessarily aggressive, income stream that you need to live a life you love.

This is the point at which wealth creation becomes more about 'playing the long game'. Reaching wealth targets doesn't necessarily mean radically changing spending habits or starting to spend up big simply because you have the means to do so. In fact, many intergenerationally wealthy families are said to be relatively conservative with their spending.

When you have a large capital base, it becomes less attractive to be constantly trying to find ways to deploy your capital to work at its maximum capacity.

You are less interested in being a hands-on investor and want to reduce the energy directed towards investing activities. You want less stress, hassle and risk, so you are happy to forgo riskier premium returns and lean more towards moderate returns.

The focus becomes - how do I preserve and protect what I have worked so hard to create? You become more conservative and want to insure against economic fluctuations.

Think of these seasons like hunger.

Your level of hunger as an inexperienced investor is often higher and maybe your approach to strategy isn't quite as sophisticated. You are generally prepared to take on more risk in the early stages of wealth creation. But as your capital base grows and you broaden your experience with investing and you get closer to the goal you have for a capital base, your hunger will shift. You won't be quite as hungry to make your capital work so hard.

I believe complacency is the enemy of success and big results. In fact, you might have heard the expression, 'the enemy of a great life is a good one.' The same is true with your investing.

In my own journey, in 2009 I had been hustling pretty hard to work whatever capital and savings we had laying around. The banks finally turned around and said, "No more." It would have been pretty easy to stop, consolidate and sit back and wait for market conditions to change. Instead, I started to look for the loopholes. Where were there other opportunities that would allow me to keep moving forward? This is what opened up opportunities in the US market for me.

It was simply asking these types of questions that became the start of a journey that opened up a whole new world of property investing I never dreamt could exist…

Part II

Blueprint for Your Pipeline

Chapter 5

Quantified Vision

Before one can build a pipeline, it is essential to know the amount of water required, the starting materials and the vision for the end result.

The key challenges for enthusiastic property investors today are that the economic conditions are becoming more and more unpredictable and there is significantly more government intervention. As a result, many property investors are standing in the wings, unsure of how to navigate the market.

In years gone by, it might have been possible to take 'a punt' on an investment property. As the cost of living has risen steeply, however, the relative cost of property to incomes is out of whack. It's now true that accumulating large volumes of property with a high percentage of bank debt is not only difficult, but risky if done without care.

Many property investors who have relied in the past on simple capital growth and government incentives to build their wealth, are now nervous with all the conflicting media reports suggesting capital gains are not sustainable.

Finally, what most investors are worried about is that we're going to be stuck working longer till we're older and greyer than we'd like to be, instead of cutting free from the workplace while we're young and healthy enough to enjoy our money.

On a brighter note, those investors that have clarity about what they want, what they are prepared to put aside towards their investing and can invest in a defensive way, will cautiously move through any periods of uncertainty.

Those with a clear vision will find suitable opportunities and will not need to take unnecessary risks to 'make up for lost time'. These few skilled investors will continue to amplify their wealth.

> *A freedom warrior believes:*
>
> *Those with a clear vision will find suitable opportunities and will not need to take unnecessary risks to 'make up for lost time'.*

These same investors will find it easy to look past the media noise and find the voices that are credible and support the property investing journey because they have absolute clarity about who they are and their ability to find investment properties that fit their objectives.

Ultimately, these property investors will create the freedom they desire in their lives sooner.

Three Essential Keys To Establishing A Quantified Vision.

1. Future Clarity

The goal might be freedom, but a big part of success is clarity of outcome. Fuzzy goals result in fuzzy actions, which means that you often miss your target.

T. Harv Eker, author of 'Secrets of the Millionaire Mind' said, "The number one reason most people don't *get* what they want is that they don't *know* what they want".

Nobody would argue against the idea that you need to know exactly what you want before you take action, but in the world of property investing, this small detail is often overlooked.

There are well-intentioned people within the property industry selling ideas of 'more is better', 'ten properties in ten years' and other such ideas which all point to the idea that 'more' is the right goal.

But what if 'more' wasn't better? What if 'more' was just more headaches? What if there was a way to accumulate the 'right' number and quality property investments? A 'minimum effective dose' for you?

I strongly believe there is no right or wrong, but it's important to question convention and decide for what purpose you are buying property.

If money is a tool, then this becomes the start of a conversation about what outcomes you want in your life. It's a case of working out how much is enough for you.

My early experiences from having invested in great, good, bad and really bad properties, are that most of the painful experiences I've had could have been avoided if I'd given some attention to the question, "What do I actually want?".

The meandering approach to wealth creation is a surefire way to dilute your investing results. If you don't have clarity around what you want, then you're inviting fate and relying on luck to get you what you need.

In 1979, a group of researchers ran a goal-setting study on the Harvard Business School graduating class to assess how written and planned-for goals effect later outcomes in life. The study occurred over thirty years and found that:

1. 83% had no goals.
2. 14% had them but didn't write them down.
3. 3% of people had goals and wrote them down.
4. Thirty years later, the 3% had earned ten times more than the 83% of the population that had no goals.

In a nutshell, being clear on the level of wealth you are trying to achieve makes it easy to then reverse-engineer the outcome. Why? Because you will naturally start to ask better questions and can get clarity on the actions that move you toward that goal and those that don't. For example, what specific types of properties will take me towards my goals?

Some people just aren't goal oriented. Goals seems silly and foreign. In the past I definitely felt that way, too. Not anymore. I realised the more concrete you can be about what you want, what it looks like, how it feels, what it smells like, the easier it is to sustain enthusiasm and continuous action towards that vision.

The other interesting idea here is that clarity around what you want means you are less likely to either overshoot or fall short of your goals.

The risk that investors face is that if they push too hard, they risk starving their lifestyle of any small pleasures and squeeze out all the enjoyment in the pursuit of riches later in life.

Of course, the other extreme is postponing the need to divert income towards investing and finding at some time in the future, they fall well short of their target.

How much capital is enough?

Now, this is obviously a multi-level question, but let me give you an insight into how you might answer this question for yourself.

First and foremost, your capital goals will vary depending on how ambitious you are and how you have defined freedom for yourself.

For some investors this could be a quite modest sum of money and for others it might be quite significant. Don't compare.

Eventually however, unless you plan to blow your money on one massive party, or sell them down to buy your groceries, you need to work out how to take all the capital that you have created and turn it into an income stream.

This is where it gets interesting.

Optimistically, an income stream on a residential Australian property with no debt is say, 5% of its value. However once expenses are deducted this falls to somewhere between 1-3%. So, to earn a decent income, you really need a massive capital base. For example, in the best case scenario, $3m in net assets might get you an income stream around $90k before tax.

If, however, you were prepared to look further afield and could consistently earn a net return of closer to 8% (as can be the case with some Australian commercial property as well as US property), then you would only need to hold net capital of say $1.1m to get the same return.

Crazy, right?

Whatever it is for you, it's not so much the dollar figure of capital that makes the difference, it's how you then can convert it into an income stream. So, the answer to the question, "How much wealth is enough?" requires you to consider, once you have your lump sum or your capital to play with, what are you going to do with it to generate an income stream?

> *A freedom Warrior understands:*
>
> *To work out the amount of wealth needed requires you to consider what are you going to do with your capital to generate an income stream.*

Let's say you want $100k in passive income in retirement from your property. This table shows you that the amount of capital you need massively varies as the rate of return goes up or down:

Net Return (income stream)	Capital needed	Potential Income Stream
12%	$833k	$100k
10%	$1m	$100k
5%	$2m	$100k
1%	$10m	$100k

Terry (not his real name) was thirty-one years old and had already accumulated ten investment properties over the previous two years. He ran a small business that was a cash cow and had managed to accelerate his borrowing to get himself started as a property investor.

At the time he came to see me he had only one goal. He wanted to get to fifty investment properties over the next four years before he hit the age of thirty-five.

While the goal itself was certainly bold and exciting, it lacked any specific reference to the impact it would have on his life. What would this mean to his finances? Why was he doing it? Why fifty properties? What would those properties look like? What level of debt would he maintain? What was his exit plan?... blah, blah, blah.

I challenged him on these things and began to flesh out not just what he wanted, but why. He wanted a family. He wanted to travel extensively. He wanted to change his car every three years, he wanted to reduce his working hours to less than ten hours a week in a decade, he wanted to sell his business.

As we mapped out a vision for the future, the goals began to change shape. It started to move away from a reference to volume of properties and more towards a focus on the size of his asset base and the income stream it should deliver.

As the goal came into focus, it was easier to understand that such a large stable of properties just wasn't needed.

The Personality Spectrum And Creating Vision

Goal setting is just taking what might be subconscious and making it concrete. For some people the task of goal setting is natural and effortless. If that's you, power to you.

For many others, it requires a little more effort. I happen to be one of the latter. In my years of working in this space though, I believe this often-quoted wisdom to be true:

> *'The quality of your life is determined by the quality of the questions you ask.'*

I'd love to attribute this quote to someone, but I'm not sure which wise guy/gal said it first.

In my own life, my experience has been that it is the quality of questions that can be the difference that makes the difference.

To assist you on this journey, I encourage you to answer the following questions, simply to promote a deeper internal dialogue.

- *What aspects of your life do you love?*
- *If money and time were ample, what do you want more of in your life?*
- *If you only had two years left to get your wealth matters in order, what would you stop/start/change?*
- *Who else might be depending on you to achieve financial success? Does your financial success affect their future?*
- *If you had the choice to work less, how would that affect you and those around you?*

If you earn a significant income, or already have a high net worth and have difficulty thinking bigger, the simplest way to approach this task is to make it a game. Perhaps ask yourself these types of questions:

- *If it were a game, what level of income stream from your property investing would cause you to make a serious life change?*
- *If it were a game, who else's world would I want to change and what would that cost? What causes do I believe in? How could I use my money to influence or change something in the world?*

In other words, if you didn't have to work because you had enough money coming in from another place, would it alter the way you live your life now, or the amount of time you give to your current business/workplace?

It is also important to recognise that the pathway to wealth isn't only about the end game. There may be important milestones along the journey that need to be captured and articulated.

In particular, changes to salary levels, important big ticket expenses, time off from your business or work, sizeable charitable donations, ad hoc expenses for your kids… basically anything that may have a financial impact over the timeframe you are setting goals for. Roll these into your vision.

2. Mapping Current Coordinates

The process of mapping current coordinates is really the careful examination of you and your relationship to money today. This extends beyond just looking at your income and balance sheet. Mapping current coordinates is an assessment of who you are and what you bring to the table. It involves looking deeply at your experience, your education around investing and the money habits you have cultivated.

We would all agree and understand that our current financial position is a function of all the micro decisions you have made in the past. That's why analysing your spending habits is such an insightful way to make meaningful change. Most people walk around in a fog when it comes to really understanding their money habits. Either they aren't interested, or it is simply too painful to consider.

I would encourage anyone who is serious about wealth and wealth creation to consider undertaking a basic analysis of how money flows in their lives. Even if you earn $500k per year, but after you take out all your living expenses, your surplus is next to nil, by definition you are living a hand-to-mouth existence. I assure you that many high-earners DO live this way.

More on being a good steward of your money and elevating your money wisdom in Chapter 12.

3. Define Success On The Journey

I enjoy hearing about people having wins in property investing.

At the same time, I often scratch my head in confusion when the property magazines hold up an investor as a success story when the properties they have bought are having little to no positive impact in the investor's life. In many cases, the investor is geared to the eyeballs and cash-flow is negligible. The success of this investor rides 100% on strong capital growth to do the heavy lifting.

If this is success, then it seems we are celebrating volume not outcome. I am not sold on this as the only measure.

So how else could you define success as a property investor?

Is it based on the number of properties you own?
Maybe, but what if they are all lemons?

Is it based on the size of your asset base?
Maybe, but what if you are in massive debt?

Is it based on how much equity you have?
Maybe, but what if you have lazy equity that is bringing in a poor income stream?

All of these are valid, but not in isolation.

For me, one measure of success is whether your investments are moving you toward or away from freedom... the freedom to spend your time, money & resources the way you want, when you want.

> *A freedom Warrior is aware that:*
>
> *One measure of success is whether your investments are moving you toward or away from freedom... the freedom to spend your time, money & resources the way you want, when you want.*

Before you start envying those who seem to own many investment properties, consider that it might be all smoke and mirrors.

Jenny ran a small boutique business in retail. She owned four investment properties which generated a net income of $80k p.a. before tax. She felt comforted by the fact that if the business went backwards, or she got sick of it, she could walk away and still maintain her lifestyle.

Mark ran a small, but lucrative IT consultancy. He had eleven investment properties all leveraged to 90% of the property values. The net cash flow from these investments each year was minus $45k before tax. Although he knew he could sell his business, he didn't believe it would give him the lump sum he had hoped for to take some time out.

Who is winning?

If you would like help with this project, go to:
http://freedomwarrior.com.au/book

Chapter 6

A Sustainable Strategy

Before the pipeline owner began work on the pipeline, he sat on the side of the hill facing the village and just thought. He thought about the slope on the hill where the pipeline would lay, the materials needed, how much water he wanted, how it would be distributed and how he would fund it.

One of the biggest mistakes I have seen budding property investors make over the years is chasing dollars in a single deal that may or may not be taking them in the direction they want to go, instead of building a game plan for the long term.

An example of this is tying up all your resources in a 'quick' development that might take 2-3 years, preventing you from taking up other opportunities.

If you can learn the ability to build a sustainable strategy, it becomes the tool that guides your decision making, stops you from getting off track, or buying the wrong assets and generally gives you a flavor of how things will unfold financially over the coming years.

If you are completely laser-like with your focus when you are building your portfolio, your results are more likely to be amplified. It's important to note that your strategy is not necessarily set in stone. It is something that you should review and tweak as life unfolds, but not something that needs regular overhaul.

If you overlook strategy, you can accumulate a portfolio of properties that don't take you to where you want to go. It's not that poor property choices can't be undone, but because property is such a large beast in Australia, these sorts of decisions can seriously lengthen your investment timeline.

Given how expensive Australian property is, it's really easy to buy one or two properties that don't quite 'fit' what you want and then become stuck. Perhaps because the banks tell you that you've 'tapped out' and hit your borrowing limit.

When it comes to property investing, it is super easy to get distracted. The deal of the decade rolls around at least weekly when you start to look for opportunities. It is as difficult (possibly more) to say 'no' to the wrong opportunities as it is to find the gems. The challenge of having a poor strategy, or not having one at all, is that it can take you further away rather than closer, to the aspirations you have.

What most business owners and executives are really concerned about is that retirement will move further into the future because their investing efforts won't give them what they need.

On the other hand, if you get the strategy piece right, then property transactions you undertake align with your goals and move you to where you want to go.

You can navigate all opportunities with a filter that allows you to easily detect if it is in alignment with your plan. This automatically means you are consciously moderating the use of your borrowing limit.

You are able to cut through all the noise and distractions surrounding the property industry. You have clarity on what you want, where you are going and how you are going to get there. This doesn't prevent you from taking advantage of opportunities as they present.

Finally, you can track your progress on any deals you get involved in and feel comfortable that the pace you are keeping will get you to the destination that you want in the quickest possible time frame.

Strategy Versus Tactics

Many people confuse strategy and tactics.

Strategy describes what you are trying to achieve and how you are going to get there. Tactics describe specific actions you could take along the journey.

Many published articles on property investing talk about tactics. What's hot, what's not, what current trends in markets look like etc. Not many step back and reflect on strategy. To their credit, they are a great source of education and tactical information, just not strategy.

Sun Tzu, an ancient military strategist wrote a book called, "The Art of War." He described that, "Strategy without tactics is the slowest route to victory. Tactics without strategy is the noise before defeat."

Both are crucial, but the average property investor uses the two terms interchangeably and so often focuses on the latest trend or hotspot to drive decision-making, rather than referencing a predetermined game plan.

A Quick Word on Superannuation

I think it's a lovely notion to entertain the idea of enjoying a long retirement, but the truth is that from a financial point of view, most people underestimate the length of time they will live and the funds they might need to make it comfortable.

Stats from ABS in 2017 tell us that the average age at retirement from the work force for persons aged 45 years and over in 2016–17 was 55.3 years (58.8 years for men and 52.3 years for women).

Perhaps you thought it was higher… maybe for some it is.

But here's the thing, even if the stats are skewed, there is no doubt that people are living longer.

According to other stats, the average life span in Australia is 82.4 years.

So for women that could mean around thirty years in retirement and just slightly less for men.

That's a lot of money needed to carry you (in style) for so long without working.

Is superannuation important? Absolutely. It is another form of savings with some great tax benefits. By itself, will it get you to the level of retirement wealth you want? Personally, I don't think so.

> *A Freedom Warrior knows:*
>
> *Superannuation is important, but by itself might not give them the level of retirement they want. Property investing is the most effective method for bridging the gap.*

The Five Essential Keys To Developing A Sustainable Strategy:

1. Set Roadmap Foundations

When it comes to developing a sustainable strategy, there is definitely not one shoe that fits every person. Everyone has their own definition of freedom and goals, their own unique risk profile, different means and different aspirations.

Having said that, in the development of your own personal strategy, it's important to decide on a few important things after you have quantified your vision:

> i) You need to be clear on the amount of current capital and future earnings you want to commit to investing over the next 3-5 years. Can you contribute a lump sum in one go, or do you need to extract it from your business/wages as you earn it? This will drive your decisions around what to buy and when. Establishing this forms the foundation of your game plan - see previous chapter for help with this.

ii) Are you going to be an investor that develops their capital base first and then tries to flick the switch into cash flow later on, or an investor who is going to pursue cash flow immediately? There is no right or wrong with any of the strategies in terms of preference, but it is important to read the economic climate in developing your tactics.

iii) Your timeline. Over what period of time do you want to set your target? It can't be too short and will largely depend on your income replacement goals and means. If you are pushing towards building your cash flow, it might be a 5-7 year outlook, while if you are focused more on building capital, then a longer outlook of 12-15 years might be more suitable.

iv) Identify any key milestones your plan should take into consideration. These might include known breaks from work, major items of expenditure, or other life events that might have a financial implication.

v) Review the buffet of available strategies and assess which ones are most likely to get you to your desired destination fastest. This should include both mainstream and alternative property investing strategies (covered in more detail in Alternative Investments - Chapter 8).

vi) Assess your risk preferences and be realistic about how much risk you are prepared to bear. There are plenty of online tools that give you a rating, but the more important exercise is thinking about your relationship to money and being committed before you deploy any money. If the thought of losing money freaks you out, weigh up opportunities where the risk of loss is extremely low and perhaps stick to local markets you know intimately.

vii) Something that most investors don't do is what I call ' future pace' their investment decisions. In fact, it is really something that should guide almost all financial decision-making. To future pace, simply means to say, "If I were to do X with my money, how would that then map into my financial future?" It doesn't have to be complex and what that does is gives you an insight into how each small decision that you make has an amplified effect over time. Even if you are terrible with spreadsheets, find someone who is good with them. Spreadsheets, when used powerfully, are an excellent tool for modelling potential decisions around your investing. If this is too hard, there are some excellent online calculators that can assist with this. Some good ones I have found are on CalcXLM: https://www.calcxml.com/calculators/bud08

viii) Decide how involved you would like to be with your investing. Some professionals might tell you otherwise, but no one cares about your money more than you do. If you want maximum safety in your investing, then you should value your ability to control your investing outcomes. If you want big results, you need to dedicate time. Property investing is the most time-leveraged method of wealth creation. There are some strategies that are more towards set and forget on the spectrum, while at the other end, other strategies are very hands-on, requiring daily input and management.

> *A Freedom Warrior knows:*
>
> *No one cares about your money more than you do.*

2. Simplify To Multiply

An important part of creating a sustainable plan is keeping it simple.

For years, I've been asking this question: "How can I simplify my property investing, so I can multiply my life and vice versa?"

Your property investing is already complex enough. You don't need to add more complexity. The secret to scaling your investing results is to make things simple again. Two things you need to simplify, so you can multiply your investing results:

1. Avoid shiny objects. Stay focused on your goals and only undertake strategies that are a step towards them. A sideways step can be expensive and waste precious time.
2. Be consciously looking for ways to leverage your time by creating systems to support the administrative tasks. Lean on other people to manage the admin and don't feel you need to do everything yourself. As your portfolio and investments grow, this task can become onerous. For example, ask your accountant to handle compliance, ask your property manager to handle all bills including rates and utilities, automate your insurance renewals or use an insurance broker, etc.

Invest it in a way that is sustainable, profitable, generous, and most of all, incredibly fun... simplify your investing, so you can multiply it.

Simplicity with your investing can bring more fun, more money and allows you to have a bigger impact.

3. Assess Properties You Have

Properties With Negative Equity

Losing money really sucks. In fact, sometimes it hurts.

Many clients have asked me when they should sell an investment that isn't performing up to their expectations or that has gone backwards. Sadly, there is no straightforward answer and every situation is different.

There are a few things to consider, but first I need to say, I'm not a huge fan of trading properties in the Australian market unless it's part of your overall strategy - mostly because it's expensive, carries more risk and can limit your ability to exploit natural rises in markets.

While it may be tempting to dump a property that's underperforming or even going backwards, it's important to make sure that the reasons for selling are extremely concrete.

If I ever thought about selling an investment property, I would consider the following:

- Is holding the property causing any impingement on your lifestyle that is putting you under stress?
- Is it draining you of cash-flow and not performing, or going backwards?
- Is holding the property affecting your borrowing capacity when you want to invest in another property?
- Can you afford to wear the cash loss right now?

If you are in that unfortunate position of carrying a property that has actually gone backwards as it's worth less than the bank loan, then you need to consider whether you can actually afford to take that capital loss or cash hit if you sold.

For most of us (apart from maybe the filthy rich), it's quite a painful thing to lose money on investments. Before you make any decision around selling an investment, whether you think it's good, bad or average, make sure you do your research.

Look at the facts. That means looking at wages growth, vacancy rates, infrastructure spending, demographics, and other factors that may have an impact on whether there's anything on the horizon that might change the outcome in the future.

Whatever you do, don't sell on a whim or for emotional reasons. I have heard of people who have sold what they have perceived to be average-to-bad investments, in the pursuit of something more exciting, and then something happened in that market and the capital growth has gone through the roof.

In other words, move slowly and deliberately. It's easy to get caught up in emotional buying and panic selling.

Every situation is different. The right decision always comes down to collecting facts (not opinions), doing your due diligence and weighing up the pros and cons.

Lazy Capital

The other thing to look for is lazy capital. Sometimes you can be holding investment properties that have had equity gains in the past, but are now not providing much/any gains or cash-flow. While a market lull is normal (markets do not increase in a straight line), it is important to be looking at whether you can use equity to springboard into other investments.

I am not a huge fan of over-leveraging (over-borrowing) if you don't need to. In fact, this could be the source of some pain for many highly-geared investors in years ahead if the market changes direction. If, however, you are defensive in your investing, one of the main advantages of investing in property over shares, is the ability to realise some of your gains, without selling the asset.

Review your properties with a professional who can help you assess this.

Interest Rate Reviews

I am truly surprised at the number of investors who rarely or never review the interest rates on loans they hold. Often banks charge people a higher interest rate on their loans simply because they are loyal and do not question their rates....and basically, they can get away with it!

A bank is an environment where the 'squeaky wheels' definitely get the best deals. Reviewing loans annually can save thousands of dollars in interest over time.

4. Adapt Your Strategy To Market Conditions

A lot of investors ask me questions on what they should do if they can't bank on high capital growth for the next few years.

I think the fact that people are asking the question of, "What else?", is fantastic in itself. I'm a huge advocate of finding opportunities to grow your wealth regardless of what the market is doing.

There are a few strategies that lend themselves to manufacturing equity and creating profit immediately. These might include small-scale developments, buying at below market value and renovations. You do have to work a little harder to find these deals, but if you can find opportunities to manufacture a decent profit straight away, then even if we go into a period of either very flat growth, or a slight decline, it provides some cushioning.

Given that lending is getting so tough and markets are flattening, you need to be widening the net of opportunities you consider if you want to keep moving forward.

If you haven't already, this is a great time to be looking at opportunities within the US market. Conservative strategies available in this market are now perfectly positioned for Australian investors to take advantage of - more on this in Chapter 8.

5. Learn when to lean on the banks

All banking systems, both here in Australia and in the US, are becoming increasingly conservative. Lending is becoming tighter and tighter in spite of low interest rates. The banks are under pressure from Governments and other regulators to alter their lending practices to control capital growth and support affordability.

The upshot of this for the average Australian investor is that they need to learn how to use the banks to their advantage or work around them.

An important part of working with banks in order to fuel your strategy is to be constantly reviewing and looking for opportunities to streamline or save money. Even if you have no interest in borrowing from the banks right now, it is a useful exercise to be fully aware of what your lending capacity looks like and how close you are to tapping out.

The metaphor that I often use is that your borrowing capacity is like a glass. As you borrow from the banks, the glass is filled with water. As it approaches the top, you need to be mindful that the property purchases that you undertake at that time are carefully selected. Once your glass is full, your borrowing capacity is reached. From here you either need to create more equity in your portfolio or generate significantly more personal income before you can go back and ask for more money.

I must mention that working with an amazing finance broker to assist with this is 100% essential for professional investors.

Another reason that US property investment strategy has become attractive is that where we hit limits with the Australian banking system, we can then either negotiate with US banks who have different criteria for lending, or we can be dealing directly with private lenders and deal makers, to access projects on a cash basis.

If you would like help with this project, go to:
http://freedomwarrior.com.au/book

Chapter 7

Elegant Execution

A monsoon was coming. Before implementing the blueprint for the pipeline, the future pipeline owner gave much thought to whether the route he'd selected was the right one and whether the team was appropriately skilled and responsive. He continued to check and recheck the calculations and research, for he could not afford for the pipeline to fail.

Our ability to assemble the bow and arrow and shoot the arrow effectively when we find suitable property deals is critical.

I regularly speak to investors who tell me they are 'chasing deals'. This might be due to an inability to find good opportunities before others, harness resources and team, or make an informed decision and then act purposefully when the right opportunities come along.

Your ability to execute elegantly is what will move you forward or keep you stuck, and yet it is given so little energy by most investors. It's not 'sexy' to prepare for the deal. In fact, most of property investors skim over this step because it seems to hold the least value.

If you get this piece wrong, you carry a high risk of making decisions to invest in property based on flimsy research, or misleading information. Without the ability to build a robust business case for each investment, you reply on hope and luck and you expose yourself to unforeseen risks.

You risk creating a fragmented team that doesn't understand you and your vision and cannot proactively harness resources, advice and information for you as you need it. This costs you real time and money.

Finally, you lack the skills to discern the good from the bad deals and risk becoming a 'deal chaser'. This biggest cost of this is that you waste precious time and energy that could otherwise be developing wealth.

Above all else, what you are really concerned about is that you'll not only miss out on great opportunities because the 'timing' was off, but that you'll fall into bad property deals you shouldn't have touched in the first place.

But it doesn't have to be this way at all.

If you understand and prepare to execute elegantly, then every investment decision is based on a calculated, predetermined criteria and solid business case. There is a much lower margin for error and major risks are mitigated.

Your team is carefully pre-screened and pre-selected. You are clear in your expectations and they 'have your back'. They are masters in their field and you feel they are capable of being part of your team not just for a single deal, but for the long haul.

You have a carefully designed system and criteria for vetting and assessing property deals. This helps you 'rule in' or 'rule out' opportunities as they come in.

Because what you really want is the peace of mind and confidence that when you move forward with an opportunity, it multiplies your wealth and takes you closer to freedom.

Three Ways To Help You Develop Elegant Execution:

1. Build A Robust Business Case

Many people understand that a single well-chosen investment property can make a massive difference to their overall financial position over time. The problem many property investors have though, is that they don't know how to weigh up opportunities.

A lot of investors don't have a strategy, so they assess property deals on the fly, using reliance on 'gut feel' alone.

As you move through the seasons toward being a professional investor, there is a shift away from relying on 'gut feel' and a move towards being very methodical about the framework applied.

Building a robust business case is not just about putting together a bunch of media reports advocating a certain area to invest in. It is a search for facts and figures, which either support or rule out a particular investment. For example, facts should be based on actual committed decisions, such as confirmed infrastructure spending, and should not rely on speculative or proposed infrastructure spending.

Other examples of things that you might consider looking at when building your robust business case are things like market sentiment, days on market, employment statistics, industry reliance, current population and projected population growth, and geographical location.

In essence, you are looking for clues on what the major drivers for potential increases in capital growth and rental yield are going to be.

2. Calculate The Cost Of Inaction

If you can start thinking in terms of opportunity cost, you immediately find it easier to make decisions around the way you spend and invest your money.

You may have heard of 'opportunity cost' before. It refers to the value of what you must give up in order to choose something else. For example, if we go on a fancy holiday to Japan, we might have to forego a large portion of the deposit on a new investment property.

No matter what we want, we must give up something else in order to get it. In our businesses, we give up time for money. We give up money for possessions. Every resource you have (money, time, land, etc.) can be traded for something else but when you make that trade, you give up the chance to trade that resource for something else.

Not many people consider opportunity cost when investing in property. The easy decision is to go for instant gratification… maybe it's the cheapest, or the lowest risk option. The harder decision is to invest in something that will yield returns in the future.

I know about the true meaning of opportunity cost first hand.

Every day I see people desperate to get into the next investment, sometimes buying properties that they haven't really thought through, or based on flimsy research.

Experience has taught me many things, including the need to plan the next move, plan for the outcomes I want in the future and only invest when all the 'boxes' I have set have been ticked.

We all have only limited capital and savings capacity. It is vital that you are clear about your investing criteria and regularly weigh up how putting money into one deal might mean missing out on another.

At the end of the day, you have no crystal ball, but understanding how to measure opportunity cost can make hundreds of thousands of dollars of difference in the future.

Many of the investors I have worked with describe having a very comfortable existence even before they began investing in property. They had decent income and a pretty good lifestyle, although maybe not as lavish as they would like.

What they all neglected to realise though, was the cost of not taking action. Over time, I have calculated the average cost of not investing in property somewhere in the vicinity of about $1.5m to $2m worth of lost wealth over a period of twelve-fifteen years.

> *A Freedom Warrior knows:*
>
> *You have no crystal ball, but understanding how to measure opportunity cost, can make hundreds of thousands of dollars of difference in the future.*

Now, this is not an estimate based on aggressive investing or heavy risk-taking. This is based on very simple, low-risk property investing modelled over that time. When you begin to calculate the cost of inaction, it becomes easy to understand the importance of taking action today.

3. Decide At What Level You Want To Play

Time is a precious commodity to everyone.

Business owners are attracted to business in the first place because they are ambitious. They don't want to work for someone else; they want to push the limits of what they can earn; and they want the potential to own their time.

Executives are ambitious by nature and many like the idea of developing wealth that reflects their ambitions at work.

When it comes to property investing, investors tend to fall into one of three categories:

The Do-It-Yourself Investor

> These are people who do their own research and like to have full control over the process. They source information from magazines, newsletters, the Internet, and other investors.
>
> With an abundance (or mountain) of conflicting information comes uncertainty. Whose opinion do you follow? Whose advice is sound? And who is just trying to sell you something? This can sometimes lead to analysis paralysis.
>
> Arguably, this can be a slow and painful way to build wealth through property, with an extremely steep learning curve and room for error. Even if you are good at it, it is definitely the slowest path.

The Done-For-You Investor

The second kind of investor seeks someone to do it for them. These people recognise that they don't have the time or the expertise to figure it out themselves, so they have to put their trust in someone.

Maybe they work with advisers or experts, go to property seminars, and hand over their money with high hopes. If they're lucky, things will go well.

The done for you model can be incredibly successful if you find the right person, as you benefit from the skill and integrity of the person you are dealing with. You hope they do the right thing by you and select a property that performs.

The Done-With-You Investor

The third kind of investor is attracted to the 'Done With You' model. This is the person who wants the balance between speed and control, but still wants to leverage other people's intellectual property and networks.

Here, you're investing alongside people who are investing for themselves as well. These mastermind groups are very difficult to find but can actually be the fast-track approach.

You stay in control. You invest alongside people who can share insights, open doors and share opportunities with you.

Conclusion?

Take the time to identify your level of experience and knowledge, appetite for risk, willingness to be coached, personality, and your goals. Then, decide which level you want to play at.

If you would like help with this project, go to:
http://freedomwarrior.com.au/book

Part III

Develop Alternative Sources

Chapter 8

Alternative Options

The local river, which had once flowed with deep waters, was now just a dry creek bed.

Over the years, the original pipeline owner had inspired many other local villagers to set up pipelines of their own. In doing this, he had recognised the need to look for opportunities further afield and across the ocean had discovered another world of pipeline building that gave him infinitely more opportunities. His game had changed again.

If you want to get wins with your investing regardless of the economic climate, then you need to consider incorporating some 'alternative investments' in your portfolio.

Property investing seems to have become a permanent fixture in the mainstream media. Everyone is talking about it as if they are an expert. Go to any barbecue and everyone (whether they have invested in property themselves or not) will have an opinion on it.

What was once the pastime of the few, is now the pastime (and passion) of many. The great news about this is that wealth is now spreading from a small minority to more people with no prior family wealth. Property investment is now accessible to anyone who has enough determination and grit. The best example of this that I've seen, is many new migrants taking on 2-3 jobs to get their foot in the property market door within a couple of years.

The bad news is that the marketplace for buying properties is now significantly more crowded, there are plenty of people exploiting the demand for owning investment properties and there is more noise and conflicting opinion about what people should do than ever.

Many property investors are nervous and are putting investing into the 'too hard' basket. Not everyone wants to spend every spare waking hour outside of work, trying to find the diamonds in the rough.

A problem Australian investors face is that the loudest voices in the property space are often offering 'vanilla' (same old), or the quality properties they offer are over-priced.

In addition, capital growth rates that were once good, regardless of what or where you bought, are now flattening or in some cases are in mild decline.

The few good deals out there are known by many and so, unless you have an inside track on a deal, gems are snatched up before they even come onto the market. It is commonly accepted now that in major capitals, if you are time poor, working with a buyer's agent is essential.

What many investors are starting to worry about, is that at a time that they want to be making their capital work hard, they will stall because they don't have the time to chase down the good deals.

Alternatively, we could be open to exploring new strategies that the average investor simply doesn't know about or has only a limited awareness of. Instead of just the choice of vanilla, we could have access to many other flavours of property opportunities.

With access to this new information we can adapt our tactics to exploit opportunities. For example, shifting our attention from a market that is struggling, to another that might be in a state of growth. In other words, we continue to grow our wealth despite market conditions.

And with this wider, more diverse set of opportunities, comes a capacity to suddenly accelerate results that might otherwise have taken many additional years to come to fruition, if at all.

> *The Freedom Warrior knows:*
>
> *If we are open to exploring new strategies that the average investor simply doesn't know about or has only limited awareness of, then instead of just 'vanilla', we could have access to many other flavours of property opportunities.*

The US Market Opportunity - A Quick Overview

Here are just some of the reasons why the US market offers unparalleled property investing opportunities:

1. It's CHEAP! The average house price there is significantly lower than in Australia so the funds required for a single deal can be relatively small.
2. You don't need to be a master of US property, the local markets or economics.
3. You can participate in the market without even needing to own the property.
4. You can massively increase your liquidity in contrast to other types of property investing.
5. You can begin investing with small amounts of capital.
6. Your ability to transact is much fast than with Australian real estate.
7. The ability to generate returns in the vicinity of 8% to 12% net is not considered unreasonable.
8. Because the cost to start playing is relatively low, you can manage your exposure.
9. Most opportunities are easily accessible to Australians.
10. There is a spectrum of strategies available which give you the ability to be as hands-on or hands-off as you choose. For example, you can participate in property deals without having to manage tenants.
11. There are few easily accessible opportunities to invest in assets in Australia that would give comparable returns.
12. There are still opportunities to participate in appreciating assets in this market, but with much lower price points for entry.

There are some US property investment strategies I simply would not recommend. This is because they are too complex, require too much time or knowledge, or access is too difficult.

The primary strategies an Australian could consider are:

1. Investing in private property funds - In a nutshell, you give your money to a fund manager and they pool your money with other private investors to buy highly vetted assets that none of us would be able to buy on our own. You then share in the returns.

Funds can be run in many different ways, but investments are generally secured against actual properties and can vary between long-term and short-term loans, as well as across many different classes of real estate. As an investor you participate in the overall returns of the fund.

2. Private lending deals - You become the bank. You lend money to a vetted borrower who generally needs the funds for a short/medium term loan to purchase/rehabilitate a property. When you make the loan, it should be secured against the property and the loan should be a conservative percentage of the home value. In the event of a default, you are protected because you are able to take possession of the home.
3. Passive turnkey lending deals - You purchase a fully renovated, tenant-ready home. May be leveraged through a bank/private lender or cash only.
4. Active turnkey lending deals - You purchase an unrenovated property and renovate to prepare it for a tenant. May be leveraged through a bank/private lender or cash only.
5. Doing deals with US locals in a joint venture arrangement, where you can earn interest plus profits can be split. It is a hybrid of a private lending deal and active turnkey. You work with a local deal maker to find a property below market value. You act as the lender and then you either sell the property on completion and split profits in addition to your interest on the loan, or you hold the property for a predefined period and then sell in the future, again for interest, plus a share of profits.

A brief overview of the pros and cons of these strategies is listed below. Bear in mind that this is not intended as a comprehensive guide and would require further education and advice from a professional and research before you undertake any of these.

STRATEGY	PROs	CONs
Lending deals	• Small capital required • Can be low risk opportunities • Lending secured against an asset • LVR generally conservative • Short term and long-term opportunities available • Returns range from 8-15% pa depending on deal • Paperwork is simple and can be administered by an independent attorney • No tenants / maintenance • You control the asset	• You must know who you are working with • If lending deal falls over, you take on the asset (which you might not want to do) • Specialised paperwork needed to articulate loan
Private Funds	• Completely hands-off • Ability to create bigger returns because they are able to access opportunities individuals can't afford. • Simple distribution of returns • Ability to reinvest profits • Less administration for entry	• Restricted entry in some cases to different times of the year • Some fund managers offer better transparency than others • Communication on performance can be limited • No guarantee that past performance will continue

	• Access to a greater cross section of opportunities - diversification • No tenants / maintenance • There are a range of fund types	• Minimum periods for investment • High reliance on fund manager's judgement
Joint Venture Deals	• Sharing the risk • A deal maker on the ground handling admin for you • Can be long-term or short-term opportunities • Ability to be creative and flexible with deal structure	• High degree of trust in JV partner • Sometimes you are locked into the deal till completion • Special contracts needed to articulate deal
Passive Turnkey	• Hands-off for investor • You are making cash-flow from day one • Ability to have independent inspection of property before purchase • Allows you to leverage in some cases	• You now have to deal with tenants (as with Aus property) • More administration to set up • Bank lending can be more restricted than for the locals if you want to refinance • High reliance on contractors, deal maker
Active Turnkey	• Manufacture profit immediately. • Allows you to leverage in some cases	• You now have to deal with tenants (as with Aus property) • More administration to set up

	• Higher degree of control over asset purchased. • Allows you to learn/be educated during the process.	• Bank lending can be more restricted than for the locals if you want to refinance • Risk of renovations being done to poor standard • High reliance on contractors, deal maker

Part of the reason that the US market is so lucrative is just that it's a completely different economic environment. Labour is significantly more affordable, transacting property is cheap and stamp duties are negligible.

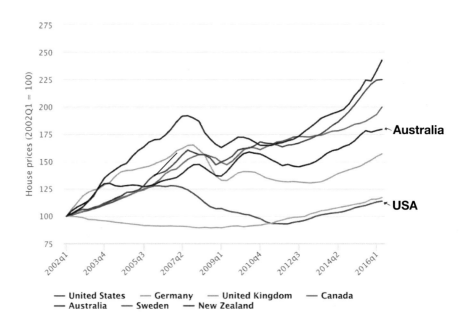

This chart was prepared by the OECD and highlights the relative discrepancy between the cost of housing in Australia and the US.

It was noted by the rest of the world after the Global Financial Crisis that even though the price of real estate dropped significantly in the US, the comparative rents did not drop much at all. This created a distortion in the market where the income stream or yield that could be generated from US real estate 'went through the roof'.

The market has pulled back from some of those crazy income streams that it had ten years ago, but relative to price, the rental income on a typical US property is still significantly stronger than what we can achieve here in Australia.

US property investing had a period of interest from Australians in 2010-2014 but has fallen out of popularity over the last few years mainly because of the fall in the Australian dollar, combined with the boom we've had here. In addition, at that time US property was perceived to be high risk.

The time has come for that perception to shift. The market has evolved, and reputable players have emerged. It is too good an opportunity not to consider as part of your investment mix.

> *The Freedom Warrior recognises:*
>
> *The world is a small place. The US market has evolved, and reputable players have emerged. It is too good an opportunity not to consider as part of your investment mix.*

Five Tips To Accessing And Thriving with Alternative Property Investing

1. Become the global citizen

One of the most critical elements of being a successful property investor is cultivating the right mindset. I strongly believe that for Australian property investors to succeed over the next decade, they must develop the mindset of being a global citizen.

Thirty to forty years ago, it was generally accepted that if you were investing in property, you would do it within your own city or suburb. In more recent times, it's the norm to invest in property interstate, sometimes sight unseen. We've come a long way. The fear of investing outside of one's suburb has been dissolved.

Most Australians look across our nation when they're considering property investment opportunities. Very few people will restrict the property investments that they undertake to the suburb, city, or state they live in.

It is inevitable that the fear of investing in other countries is eventually going to become a limiting factor.

I believe there are still stellar opportunities available within the Australian market, but the US market offers a completely new set of opportunities, which can be used in parallel with what we have here in Australia.

Given our steep property prices, bank lending challenges and the economics of the Australian property market right now, it is wise to be looking for alternatives in order to continue to grow during what might become an economic winter here.

It's perfectly understandable that Australians may have a fear of taking their money offshore, or of investing in an environment where they are unfamiliar. But... what is unfamiliar can become familiar through education and exploration.

We are definitely a nation where consensus rules, especially when it comes to property investing. Many are studying what others are doing in order to determine their own actions. The downside of this is that if we're waiting to see what others do before we take the plunge, then often we've either missed the boat, or we're chasing the market.

The concept of being a global citizen simply means that you are open to opportunities, regardless of where they reside.

> *The Freedom Warrior knows:*
>
> *The concept of being a global citizen means that you are open to opportunities, regardless of where they reside.*

The world is becoming a smaller and smaller place. International travel is becoming easier and much more affordable. Here in Australia (although more restricted), we no longer reserve the Australian property market just for Australians, and neither do many other nations.

International property investing seems to be the last mental obstacle that many Australians see when they're thinking about their property investing. There are already a large number of Australians that invest in the US share market. However, the number of Australians that have been open to investing in the US property market has been significantly smaller.

At the beginning of the Global Financial Crisis, when the property market in the US first collapsed, interest in the US property market was high from all over the world. Unfortunately, because the environment was unfamiliar, a lot of people dived in head first and unfortunately got some cuts and bruises in the process.

The good news is that over the last decade or so, understanding of the opportunities and the environment have become significantly more sophisticated and the astute investor can now access that market in a much more structured and safe way.

Why don't many Australian professionals advocate US property?

It is not well understood by many. At best, people understand the strategy of just buying homes and this is often fraught with property management challenges.

It's hard to make money as an adviser in this space. Many are consultants or wholesalers.

There have been many stories of people being burned in the past.

We don't know who to trust over there.

Money invested in the US reduces the pool of money that most advisers want you to put into their own products and the share market.

2. Find Inefficient Markets

You can always make money if people are slow to see the opportunity, or if an asset is priced below what it is really worth. This is called market inefficiency and it's what allows people to make money from it.

As I've already stated, the major issues with conventional property investing here in Australia is that it's expensive and everybody is on to it.

For every strategy that exists in the Australian property market, there are advisers, buyers' agents, real estate agents, property resellers, builders and educators who are trying to get you to believe that their strategy is the one and only right strategy.

Regardless of what strategy you adopt, it's clear that people are interested in property investing because we no longer believe that the government will be able to look after us in retirement and we want to take our financial future into our own hands.

If we consider that a large volume of alternative opportunities exists in the US, it's important to understand why they are so appealing to property investors.

Firstly, because of the volume of people interested in property here in Australia, our market has become relatively efficient. What that means is that the opportunity to exploit the market here and make rapid gains is much smaller, hence harder. Also, the government and banks are adding their own hand brakes to the market.

In contrast, the US market remains relatively inefficient. This has evolved because of its size, the nature of the economy, low wages and the fact that each state has its own set of rules and regulations.

What that means for the average investor is that there are many opportunities to exploit that inefficiency and make significant returns.

Finding markets where the inefficiencies are the greatest is an opportunity to grow our wealth.

3. Blend To Amplify

The Australian property market has historically been awesome at helping you build a capital base.

The problem now though, is that investing in assets that grow in value but don't produce much cash-flow is fine when we don't need the cash, but at some point we need our assets to start paying us. We need a decent income stream. If we don't achieve this, it means we are forced to sell assets in retirement to survive.

The primary reason for investing is US real estate opportunities is to begin to turn the dial from capital building to cash flow building. In other words, income replacement.

> *The Freedom Warrior is aware:*
>
> *Investing is US real estate opportunities helps turn the dial from capital building to cash flow building. In other words, income replacement.*

With the Australian property investing space becoming crowded and borrowing much tougher, it is a no brainer to begin blending Australian property with specific US property investing strategies.

Having been an investor in US property for a decade now, I've certainly had a lot of small cuts and bruises as I have learned about the market. What I've come to understand is that there are opportunities over there which are as concrete and as lucrative as the opportunities that we have here in Australia…but you need to find the right people to work with.

I'm an advocate of blending the best of what's available in Australia and in the US, because I recognise that strategies that worked here in the past aren't necessarily going to work now.

If you want to continue to grow over the next three to five years, it is more important than ever that you start to think outside the square. That means looking at new opportunities and new ways of investing your money. During a period when most other property investors are going to be floundering, the US offers a variety of strategies that are suitable for the astute Australian investor.

Is it for everyone?

Definitely not. It is for ambitious people that want to bring an edge to their investing. It is for people who recognise that having a strong income stream from another source would be a game changer for them. It's for people who are tired of waiting for their capital assets to start producing an income here.

4. Understand the metrics between markets

Apart from the fact that property has become incredibly expensive in Australia, the market is slowing and there is government intervention to discourage investors, there is one more uncomfortable reality for Aussies... the banks are being painful with their lending.

So even if you wanted to argue that an Australian investment property will always outperform the cash return achievable in the US market, the reality is that many Australian investors are butting up against the banks not wanting to lend any more money, unless you have a massive income to back it.

Australian property experts will tell you that our property market moves in cycles, and that eventually, the market will rise again. They will tell you that property is a long-term strategy and that you should never sell to time the market.

I agree with all of that...

AND...

...the reason we invest in capital assets is partly so that one day we can generate a strong cash flow. It is NOT because one day we hope to sell down one asset at a time so that we can live off the capital - that's the path to blowing up wealth.

> *The Freedom Warrior knows:*
>
> *The reason we invest in capital assets is so that one day we can generate a strong cash flow. It is NOT because one day we hope to sell down one asset at a time so that we can live off the capital - that's the path to blowing up wealth.*

What bothers me is that even if you are sitting on a huge capital asset base in Australia, outside of commercial real estate, the income stream is crappy. As mentioned earlier, a good gross yield on residential is 4-5%, but after expenses it falls to 1-3%.

To go back to our earlier example, imagine we own a one-million-dollar property in a blue chip area and that we get just above the average Australian gross yield of say 4%. By the time you take out your costs, that can drop as low as 1%.

Do you think earning 1% on your million-dollar investment is a reasonable return?

Hopefully you are saying no.

My feeling right now in the market is if you're doing the same old strategies and earning anywhere from 1%-3%, maybe even 4%, you're really doing yourself a disservice.

Now is the time to be considering alternative strategies where you can boost cash flow.

In an ideal world, particularly if we look over what has occurred in the last two decades, there is a strong case to use the Australian property market to 'pump up the tyres' and build your capital base. You could make do with the fact that the cash flow would be limited or next to zero and once your capital base had reached the level that you felt satisfied with, then you could be looking to redeploy that capital into higher-yielding (higher-income) assets.

This is where the blending idea becomes important. I would never be advocating you go all in on any one strategy (see Chapter 10 - Protected Navigation), but by 'dipping your toe' into new and lucrative strategies, your game plan could be accelerated.

Our options

If we're examining the Australian market, and we feel that we're entering a period of limited growth (capital gains), then we have one of three options.

1. Do nothing and ride it out - For many investors this is completely fine, especially if our asset base is where we want it and there is little risk of vacancy or rents falling. Unless you rock the boat with the banks, they generally leave you alone.
2. We can identify assets that allow us to manufacture forced appreciation upfront - This might include renovations, developments, undervalued assets etc. A good strategy if you can get the lending and have the time and relationships in place to find these deals.
3. We can seek opportunities that generate cash flow - The US property market offers exceptional opportunity for this.

As described earlier, here is another illustration of the power of considering alternatives:

Let's say you want an income from a property of $100k.

To do that in the Australian market and assuming no debt, you would need to hold roughly $4m in net assets to achieve this after expenses (assume a 2.5% net yield).

To achieve that in the US market, assuming a more conservative yield of 8%, this would only require assets of $1.25m.

Enough said.

5. Dip Your Toe In First

I am NOT advocating you go all in on US property, but you might blend the best of both worlds.

Investing in the US property market is no longer as wild an idea as it used to be, but as with everything new, we need to tread carefully.

Who you work with in this market can make or break your investment experience, as I have experienced first-hand. Only work with 'A' grade players. Anything less becomes a gamble.

Take your time to assess the calibre of the people you deal with and speak to like-minded investors who are on a similar journey.

Above all else, be defensive at all times (see Chapter 10 - Protected Navigation).

If you look at all of these alternative options and you run them through the filters from Chapters 5-7, you will accelerate your results.

If you would like help with this project, go to:
http://freedomwarrior.com.au/book

Chapter 9

Mindful Diversification

The Pipeline owner was getting worried. He had initially thought he was imagining things, but there was no doubt now that the river bed was receding. Too many neighbours had built competing pipelines. The time had come to start searching for sources of water further afield.

The theory behind diversification is to not 'put all your eggs in one basket', but, in plain English, to spread the risk.

Most people immediately think of geography when they think of diversification. In my experience, people don't really give this much thought and think if their investment properties are spread in different locations, then that box is ticked.

If you get the diversification piece wrong, you can either create unnecessary drag in your investing results, or chase returns in one market and expose yourself to unexpected market changes. We saw plenty of people do the latter in the mining boom and bust.

In the pursuit of 'being diversified', I've seen with people who buy investment properties in an unfamiliar market. This has led to the demise of those who hadn't done enough research before they purchased, or bought on the basis of someone else's flimsy research.

Another mistake is when investors who sacrifice returns for perceived safety. While in theory this might make sense, it has also been the cause of 'an average to below average' return for many people.

At the root of all these problems is the worry that a wrong move could jeopardise the hard work and results created to date, or worse, be the cause of financial ruin.

On the flip side, if you are calculated about how you diversify, you can reap the fruits of good returns in multiple markets with different drivers and economic conditions.

You can also execute decisions to invest in markets which might not be completely familiar, but with good due diligence, access opportunities that are a 'fit' for you and your risk appetite.

Also, given that diversification isn't just about geography, when you invest in property deals that you understand, there is an ability to diversify across strategies, markets or based on the team or deal maker you work with.

Ultimately, we want the assurance that we are shielded as much as possible from any downside, while trying to maximise the upside.

Three Ways To Diversify With More Mindfulness

1. Consider Diversification Beyond Geography

The average Joe thinks that diversification in property investing means buying in different places. Diversification isn't just about geography.

If diversification is about reducing risk, there are other elements to consider.

> *The Freedom Warrior recognises:*
>
> *Diversification isn't just about geography. It is about reducing risk.*

It could also be about trying to select assets that will be in different sub-markets or markets, in different cycles, employing different strategies and potentially different types of property, relying on different economies, and different property managers.

If this is true, then mindful diversification is about weighing up the strength of an opportunity and deciding if there is a way to get more of the good stuff without risking too much.

A simple example: Perhaps there is a suburb you love that ticks all your boxes for due diligence. Perhaps you buy a house and a townhouse as a way to diversify some of the risk. This would result in two different types of tenants, at two different price points.

2. Diversify Only To Reduce Risk

When done well, diversification is about trying to identify the potential risks in a market and then buying assets in a way to minimise exposure to those risks.

The problem with traditional theory on diversification is that if you aren't careful, you can accidentally kill the potential returns you could have made simply because you spread purchases between good and not so good investments.

There are some investors who have been wildly successful because they saw an opportunity in a single market and went all in. I personally know many investors who bought 100% of their portfolio in one town or city and have made big returns.

An example of this was a couple who purchased twenty homes in a single suburb located opposite a major university. They personally managed the properties as student accommodation and made a significant income across the properties. Their world-view was that there was reduced reliance on one tenant, they could control the management and detect issues early and they were capitalising on an opportunity that was unlikely to be harmed by an economic downturn.

Does this mean we should all buy up big when we see a good opportunity? To be frank, it depends on your appetite for risk and your ability to weigh up the risk in the market.

I personally don't have the stomach for this and for the novice investor, I would highly recommend against this kind of strategy.

3. Diversification Becomes More Critical Approaching Winter

In our 'seasons' model presented earlier, it was clear that as you ascend through the seasons of investing, the desire to put assets at risk diminishes. This is especially true when you consider the transition to the winter season (as described in Chapter 4).

When we become a 'winter' investor, the focus shifts to preservation and securing a reasonable rate of return, instead of chasing big returns for more risk.

Prior to this point in time, you have a higher ambition for making gains and so diversification is less of an issue. Perhaps as a newer investor, you may be prepared to take more risk to make bigger returns in the short term, with the view that if it doesn't go according to plan, you have time to recover.

Recognise the season you are in and use this to guide decisions around the intensity of diversification. If you really believe in a strategy or an area, find ways to diversify risk through other elements.

If you would like help with this project, go to: http://freedomwarrior.com.au/book

Chapter 10

Protected Navigation

In travelling beyond the village to explore new sources of water, the pipeline owner was careful to verify not only the calibre of the water source, but also the locals he needed to rely on to help him negotiate with the local landowners.

As my exploration of property investing has evolved, I realise now that there is a whole world of opportunity out there that many people have never even heard of. Some of the strategies described in this book are a sample of these.

For some people, the opportunities that exist outside of Australia may initially seem daunting. Everything is new and unfamiliar. Their perception may even be that the opportunities are risky, simply because the environment is not one they've grown up with.

The biggest problem with navigating a new opportunity in an unfamiliar environment is that it's difficult to understand what's important. There can often be conflicting information and things that you just don't know about.

We can put our faith in the wrong people. It's easy in an unfamiliar environment to rely heavily on the opinions of others, or on superficial research. In many instances, this seems like the easy way out because there is no clear checklist to run through.

Finally, we can misunderstand or miscalculate numbers, or perhaps hit unexpected hassles in managing the investment.

If we're honest, what worries us about all of this is that taking on an investment in an unfamiliar environment may result in a loss.

On the other hand, if we were methodically educated about this new environment, it would cease to be unfamiliar. With the right framework, we could begin to assess a broad cross-section of opportunities because we know how to ask the right questions and do the right checks.

We could develop a process for vetting the people you deal with to ensure that they are ethical and suitably qualified to work with.

Education can assist in helping us understand how to interpret key numbers when looking at different types of investments.

The truth is, in an ideal world, what we'd all really love is the ability to behave as a global citizen and access the best possible property investments regardless of where the investments are located.

Three tips On Navigating (Any) Property Market Defensively

1. Stack The Odds In Your Favour

There are hundreds of property experts and businesses that have sprung up to influence investors toward buying decisions that may or may not be in their best interest.

There are a number of things that investors should consider to 'stack the odds' in their favour, and essentially mitigate many of the common pitfalls associated with the property market. 'Stacking the odds' is about identifying risks and mitigating them as much as possible.

Commonly perceived risks of investing in property include:

What if there is no capital growth in the future?
Will I get a reasonable tenant?
Will I have headaches around maintenance?
What if I have a period of vacancy?
What if interest rates go up?
What if the government abolishes negative gearing?
What if I have a vacancy?

All of these risks are real, but can be massively reduced by making sure you:

- Put a plan in place BEFORE you buy anything.
- Stress test all your decisions before you buy, to make sure that any risk is acceptable.

- Think about investing in properties that will endure and be popular regardless of market conditions.
- Work with people who have reputations for excellence.
- Have a plan to reduce debt.
- Develop a plan to boost cash flow when you get to the capital level you want.
- Keep cash reserves.
- Don't take on properties that might stress your lifestyle.

The upside of property investing can be significant, but to overlook the risks is also a danger.

2. Be Defensive In Times Of Uncertainty

Markets have long been driven by greed and fear. An astute investor is aware of this and is watching for signs of both.

I am constantly having conversations with people (often non-investors) about whether the property market is going to plummet in the coming few years.

Is there going to be a repeat of the Global Financial Crisis, but this time in Australia?

I am not into crystal ball predictions, but I believe that while market undulation will always occur, a property 'crash' is highly unlikely.

My two cents is that a defensive approach always pays, especially in times of uncertainty.

> *The Freedom Warrior is aware:*
>
> *A defensive approach to property investing always pays, especially in times of uncertainty.*

It is reported by the ABS that about 1/3 of all Australian property is owned outright, while another 1/3 of property have very little debt. These two factors combined create a terrific safety net for us. As a nation, we hate debt, and are quick to pay it off where we can.

Here's what I do suggest:

- If you want to play a more defensive game with wealth, reduce or eliminate exposure to high risk/speculative properties. These might include properties with high gearing and poor cash-flow, or properties located where there is high reliance on one industry or one employer.
- If you carry a lot of personal debt (car leases, credit cards, personal loans) get rid of them as a priority.
- Don't let fear or greed drive your investment decisions.
- Keep cash reserves that equate to a minimum of 4 months property and living expenses.

Imagine if the world-wide property market did take a tumble and 20% was wiped out tomorrow. People still need to live somewhere. When the US market crashed during the Global Financial Crisis and in some cases properties lost more than half their value, the big surprise was that rents barely moved at all. In fact, rental demand went up.

The defensive investor would position themselves to hold investments that would still be sought after, even in the event of a crash.

This might mean you avoid property that is too far above or below the median house price. Overly expensive properties might experience a drop in rents if the economy went pear-shaped. At the other end of the spectrum, if you become a 'slum lord', you expose yourself to a higher level of tenancy issues. Note, I am not talking about affordable housing here.

The best defence is to always make sure your 'sleep at night' factor is high, by not investing in anything that causes you to wake up worrying.

Playing a defensive game is completely subjective, but give it some attention.

3. Assess Environment

One of the biggest mistakes that people make when they're going into a new environment is trying to focus on the deal and completely neglecting the environment.

You want to grow your experience with investing, but at the same time be safe.

As you start to examine the intricacies of the US market, you will immediately recognise that the depth and breadth of the strategies are far greater than in our market. This is partly because of the way that their economy has evolved, but quite simply, the US has made it far easier to transact property purchases, without all the messy paperwork and taxes that we have here in Australia.

In addition, the flexibility of the tax and legal system there has created loopholes and opportunities that we just could never have in Australia. All this is excellent for the astute investor that is prepared to look beyond what is familiar.

Many investors believe that in looking to undertake investments in the US market, the major consideration is tax, paperwork and administration.

I can tell you right now, these are minor hurdles and certainly not where I'd be focusing my energy if I were exploring this market.

If I were starting from scratch, the bulk of my efforts would be on the careful examination of WHO I was going to do business with. It is almost impossible to look at investing the US market without relying on a local deal maker, unless of course, you are happy to fly over there and camp out for a year or two.

In any big pond there are lots of sharks. Our goal as an astute investor is: how do you tell the dolphins (helpful!) from the sharks?

It all boils down to our capacity to do good due diligence.

Obviously, you need to investigate the opportunity, the risks and how it all works, but above all else, you need to know who you are working with.

Examples of the types of questions I would be exploring:

- Proof that they invest in their own deals themselves.
- How did I find them? Is the referral reliable?
- Evidence of results?
- Are they happy to provide reference checks?
- Can you see and review (selected by you) recent deals?
- Are they open about good and bad results?
- How long have they been in business? (Preferably in business prior to GFC.)
- Who (if relevant) do they use as subcontractors? Are they on staff?
- Do they work with foreign investors?
- Can they facilitate an introduction to a local bank?

It is really important that you develop your own set of criteria and use it.

Being cautious in new markets is critical. As an investor, it is unrealistic to believe you can be a master across all property investing strategies. In fact, even most professional investors tend to find a formula for success and then stick with it.

Getting to know a new environment will take time, but if you are methodical, it will be significantly less daunting and can pay massively over the long term.

If you would like help with this project, go to:
http://freedomwarrior.com.au/book

Part IV

Be The Captain

Chapter 11

A Robust Rudder

As the pipeline owner prepared for his imminent death, he celebrated the wisdom he had seeded in his sons and daughters and knew the legacy of the pipeline would endure for generations to come.

Creating wealth is an admirable goal. Done well, it demonstrates all the key qualities of a warrior; expanded awareness, courage, discipline, cunning, and patience.

For many investors though, the pursuit of wealth for our own ends is only part of our motivation. There is a desire to see our family, tribe, friends, community and beyond benefit from the fruits of our efforts.

And what about when we're gone?

Do we want to see our wealth trickle further downstream? If so, we want to be sure we design a plan to allow those we care about to help steer our wealth forward. We need to design a 'robust rudder' to help guide our resources to the destinations we desire while we are still around. If not, it is more than likely that others will make that call for us.

The idea of creating a legacy in whatever form, whether it is because we've sparked a great idea or have simply been a catalyst for change through our wealth, is an important element on our journey of wealth creation.

Now, if you read this and think, "Nope... don't have any interest in leaving any money behind after I am dead... gonna spend the lot," then by all means, skip this chapter. But for the vast majority of us, using our wealth to change the course of the future matters, and if it were within our power to do so, we would.

The relative scale of what we leave behind doesn't matter. Maybe we just want to help our kids out, or we want to create an everlasting legacy for the family, or perhaps we might want to make an impactful financial contribution to causes we care about… or maybe we just want to leave it to our beloved pets (you never know!).

We might be worried that our kids won't have the same opportunities that we've had. The relative cost of property and life itself seems to be getting skewed towards crazy prices, with the median house price drifting towards $1m at a rapid rate.

Perhaps we are unsure how to equip our loved ones with the skills to maintain the wealth we hope to pass on to them someday, especially if they are pursuing careers that have little relationship to business or money.

We might also be super passionate about certain causes but concerned about how to contribute in a way that is impactful, rather than just a token gesture.

And perhaps what worries us the most is that we will put all this effort into building all this wealth and we are unsure if it will be frittered away.

But, if you take action now and get on the front foot, it's possible to stay at the forefront of wealth opportunities which we can share with our family.

You can share philosophies and frameworks with your loved ones that teach them how to cultivate and grow wealth that endures and which gently and organically educates them over time.

> *The Freedom Warrior knows that:*
>
> *It is important to share philosophies and frameworks with loved ones to teach them how to cultivate and grow wealth that endures.*

It is possible to find pathways to contribute in your community and to causes you believe in to create change.

Because ultimately what many of us want is to design a legacy which allows our wealth to flow in the way we want, for maximum endurance.

Three Keys To Developing Freedom Warrior Kids Within A Family:

1. Educate, nurture and then educate some more

Building a massive asset base by itself won't necessarily create legacy.

Something that's worrying a lot of middle-aged people is: how are they going to pass their wealth on, or educate their children about money and wealth matters?

For many, making enough money to retire and live a happy life is just one motivation. Many are thinking beyond that and contemplating how to make sure that they can also help their children be good stewards of their money.

There is a lot of discussion right now about how in the next decade there's going to be one of the largest transfers of intergenerational wealth from parents to their kids..

What's interesting is that the incoming generation, or the Gen Ys, the millennials and beyond, have a very different attitude to money. There's a much stronger awareness of wanting to enjoy money now and they often give a lot of money away to help other people. The need for delayed gratification is not a familiar habit for this incoming generation.

Many studies have highlighted that a common trait amongst families who have held wealth through multiple generations is a focus on teaching kids the concept of delayed gratification. That not everything should be instant or enjoyed right now. There is also emphasis on the responsibilities that come with money.

Often, families have worked incredibly hard to earn the wealth they have and they want to make sure that the people who inherit our wealth also take good care of it.

The process of educating your children should start from a very young age, including showing them how to have a good relationship with money and to cultivate great money habits.

The decision to tell your kids, or loved ones, what you are really worth and what inheritance is coming their way is a personal preference. Some people choose to leave this till their kids are older and can understand the gravity of it. Other people choose not to tell their kids specifics around money and inheritance because they want their kids to make it on their own.

Money is a complex topic, but if you can at least start having those sorts of conversations within the family, you're going to be in a much better position than if you leave it and just hand over the fortune tomorrow.

Investing in games, books and programs which develop good money habits and attitudes from a young age will develop money skills

Have occasional family conversations around everyday topics such as how to save money, how you manage money, prioritising spending, investing, property versus shares, etc.

2. Develop A Family Charter

A family charter is a simple document that families can prepare together which articulates how they would like to see the family resources and money managed and spent. Even from a young age it can be a great tool to begin involving kids in the ideas of money management and wealth.

It is normally used where there is a family business or alike that extended members of the family need to be involved in. It is also a great tool for enrolling kids into the idea that they can contribute to the wealth of the family over time.

In some cases, people have used these kinds of family charters to make big investment decisions as a family collective, even when the kids are grown up and able to contribute financially to some investing decisions.

The main reason for developing a document like this when your kids are young, is it gives the insight into how money is managed in real life.

Even from a young age you can be documenting ideas on family holidays, setting goals and talking about basics like savings. By including kids in investing decisions, even small ones, you begin to give them a sense of participation and responsibility.

The family charter can include whatever ideas you have about looking after the 'family money' (obviously you don't need to show them everything). You can even simplify and make it a small lump sum that you collectively invest together each year. For example, for younger kids, you might have them research and participate in the investment of a few hundred dollars.

Headings to consider including might be:

1. How often you meet
2. Family values
3. What kinds of assets you like/don't like
4. How profits will be used
5. How the kids can participate
6. The rules of family money
7. How you might save towards bigger investments
8. How often you eat out
9. Budgeting

Etc, etc.

You can be as creative as you like, but bear in mind that this is not a legal document. Use it to teach good stewardship and your money values.

3. Teach Kids To 'Earn' Not 'Expect'

One of my own personal frustrations is when people tell me that their kids don't value money, but in the same breath, they reveal that they don't let their kids want for anything.

Many families want the best for their kids, but inadvertently weaken their money skills by teaching their kids to ask for anything and everything they want.

Regardless of whether you believe you 'can afford it', one of the most impactful things you can teach your children is how to be financially independent.

That's not to say you don't help them out, but by creating some level of anticipation, developing discipline and forcing them to experience delayed gratification, you can begin to teach them habits that will endure for a lifetime.

It is particularly important to be aware of when you are projecting your own money hang-ups onto your children. For example, would you rather give your child every toy they could ever dream of, simply because you didn't have those as a child? Alternatively, would you rather teach them to accept they can't always have everything they want, when they want it?

There is no right or wrong. It is simply important to be aware that your actions teach your kids directly and indirectly about how to relate to money.

The degree to which you cultivate the idea of getting kids to 'earn' what they want in your home in entirely up to you. There are no hard and fast rules and you can be as creative as you like. For example, when your child wants a big-ticket item (such as a car), there are many ways you can help them get what they want. For example, you can split the cost, you can co-save, you can set behavioural targets, you can add chores etc.

If you choose to give your child everything they want because you can't bear the idea that they might go without, ask yourself how you might feel when they are independent adults with no ability to manage their own money.

If you would like help with this project, go to:
http://freedomwarrior.com.au/book

Chapter 12

Elevated Money Wisdom

The pipeline owner recognised the need to be a good steward of his money. Not only did his family depend on it, but so too did his future unborn descendants.

Money habits not only set the foundation for your capacity to create wealth, but also how you keep it... so don't underestimate the need to improve your ability to be a good steward of your money.

Wealthy people think differently. If we want to achieve financial freedom, then we need to learn to step up our level of thinking.

It just isn't enough to make a fortune. You also need to learn how to keep it. As discussed, this includes becoming a teacher to others within your family on how to be good stewards themselves.

Good money habits are how wealth is created, but there are also plenty of instances where even wealthy people can lose massive fortunes due to poor money habits. Perhaps you've heard of families where the grandparents have created massive wealth, the parents spend it all, and the grandkids are left to start from scratch again.

This is all complicated by the fact that people don't live as hermits. There are often multiple personalities within a family, with different habits and attitudes. For example, even if you have one person in a marriage that is poor with money, the efforts around wealth creation and money stewardship can be undermined or diluted depending on whose habits are stronger.

In reference to the journey of building wealth, the more awareness and attention we can bring to the stewardship of our money, the more ease we will experience on our path to freedom.

> *The Freedom Warrior appreciates:*
>
> *The more awareness and attention we bring to the stewardship of our money, the more ease we will experience on our path to freedom.*

The key challenge that many of us face is having a desire to grow our wealth, but feeling unable to curb some of the poor money habits we've cultivated throughout our life. We might rationally recognise bad habits but struggle to change old patterns.

We might also feel torn between the decision to enjoy life now versus investing for the future. Many people behave and live life as if they have plenty of time left to sort out finances in the future. Sometimes life events can shape and influence our feelings around which is the bigger priority. Many people with a tendency to spend more for the now believe the future will take care of itself, or genuinely feel pressure to maintain certain lifestyle habits.

Sometimes even if we have a high income, if we carry some poor habits regarding the stewardship of our money, then the journey to financial freedom can feel like driving with the handbrake on.

Ultimately, the nagging feeling that many investors don't voice is that the higher income that they have worked so hard to achieve is not accompanied by a proportionate higher net wealth, or a feeling of ease.

It doesn't have to be that way, though.

If you get it right, you can adopt a money management framework that can undo years of poor money habits.

As you begin to understand the implications of different investment decisions over time, you can strike the most effective balance between lifestyle and investing for you.

On the path to financial freedom, if your money mindset strengthens and this leads to a healthier relationship with money, then ultimately this starts to speed up the process of wealth creation because you have removed one of the biggest sources of friction.

Finally, you start to feel great that your income fuels the wealth creation engine you've built, speeding up results, propelling you closer to the freedom you want.

Five Ways To Support Elevated Money Wisdom:

1. Bring consciousness to your spending

Most of us are not conscious about the money habits we have.

It doesn't necessarily matter what level of income you are on, there is a significant number of people who have no awareness or connection to their spending habits.

I ask all my new clients to rate their ability to manage money out of ten. Majority of people will rate themselves highly, but upon closer inspection, recognise there are many money 'leaks' in their habits and thinking.

One of the most useful ways to assess your capacity to be a good steward is to reverse engineer your surplus. This exercise requires you to reconcile what you think you are saving with what you are actually saving.

The way to approach this task is to list out on a weekly basis what you believe you are spending, annualise it, and then deduct it from the after-tax income you know you get. What most people establish almost immediately is that there is a gap between the two figures.

This exercise uncovers the fact that most people have very little awareness of where the money flows. There is often a massive discrepancy between the level of projected savings, based on their cursory understanding of where money flows, and the actual savings. It's not untypical for many people that bring in a good income to have only small sums of money sitting in surplus.

The purpose of the exercise is to, first of all, highlight that there is the discrepancy and secondly, give you an opportunity to identify where the leakages are. Once you've established that, there are some simple things that you can put in place to strengthen your money management practices.

Even if money management is not perceived to be a high priority for you, it is an interesting exercise to look at how small tweaks to the way that you manage your money can have a massive impact over time.

I highly encourage you to run this exercise regularly to determine where the 'slippages' in your spending are. Even if you can afford to spend big, the decision to save versus spend should be a conscious one, not accidental.

2. Automate to over-ride habits

The simplest, more overlooked money advice given by wealthy people is, "Live within your means."

Some people beat themselves up though, when (like dieting) they are unable to stick to strict budgets.

Quite frankly, budgets are hard work and it's too easy to cheat.

The easiest way to instantly improve your money management is to impose structure and automation. Automating the flow of money after it hits your personal bank accounts will give you immediate feedback on how well, or badly, you are living within your means

I've read numerous books on money management over the years and while I have found many of them inspiring, I eventually created my own hybrid system. I have been using it myself for at least a decade. I have always called it 'Gorilla Tactics with Money' (not sure why…just like gorillas 😊). Once the basics are in place, you can start to adapt it to add in additional savings accounts for specific goals.

It's really simple, but I've literally had grown men cry when I take them through this because they've been unable to break the cycle of reliance on credit cards.

I once did it as a blog, so go check out the video here: http://freedomwarrior.com.au/gorillatactics

Note to all the tight wads (on spending money and guilt):

Some people struggle to enjoy their money even when they have it.

No doubt this comes from a deep-seeded pain from their past, or habit taught by their parents which lead to feelings of guilt around spending.

Something I encourage you to embrace is the idea that if you have put a system in place to support the flow of money in your life, then be free with the spending within those rules.

I occasionally meet people who are into being super-thrifty. There is nothing wrong with this if there is a purpose. The purpose of creating wealth is to step towards feeling free and without constraints. In order to achieve this, you do need to cultivate the art of knowing when to use your money to bring pleasure.

The money that you put aside for pleasures. Spend it. If you don't cultivate the habit of enjoying your money now, its purpose and value later in life will be diluted and you might never feel you have 'enough'.

For some light entertainment that will shock you, go watch 'Extreme Cheapskates' clips on Youtube.

3. Study the money habits & attitudes of the wealthy

I speak with many people who earn a considerable amount of money. What intrigues me the most is that they too are asking questions about world economics, what the government is doing and what might happen in the economy.

They too have money pain.

My main observation though, is that they are not so much worrying about it, but more exploring how to position themselves to defend their wealth and work out how to find opportunities where others aren't looking.

And that right there, is what we should be doing regardless of our wealth level.

Wealthy people pursue knowledge with passion. Self-made wealthy people love reading. One study quoted that it is the number one habit to adopt if you want to become wealthy.

Another study found that 85% of self-made wealth people read books that help them grow, including topics like careers, biographies of successful people, self-help, health, current events, psychology, and leadership.

Here are some interesting qualities that have been published describing common traits of super wealthy people. They:

- Are not impulsive.
- Recognise the difference between wants and needs
- Focus on the long-term goals.
- Have multiple sources of income.
- Automate investing
- Are prepared for emergencies.
- Only invest in what they understand.
- Keep track of expenses.

- Live below their means.
- Are willing to make sacrifices.
- Don't get into debt.
- Pay for advice.
- Educate themselves.
- Run the numbers before making a decision.

4. Be fierce about wealth

Dwayne Johnson is someone who came from a very poor background and found himself homeless at the age of 14. One of the things that he has shared on his story was that he just decided to get angry about getting results.

Now, the way that I interpret this is that you need to be fierce about what you want. If you're passionate about creating freedom in your life, then you have to be fierce about your investing and results.

That doesn't necessarily mean that you have to obsess or spend a lot of time doing it, but if you have a low intensity of expectation, or maybe you're just lukewarm in your effort, how can you possibly expect to get outstanding results?

If you want to achieve the sort of results that outperform mediocre, then you have to have a fire in your belly.

Whether you're very extraverted about it, or whether you're more introverted about it like me, my suggestion to you is ignite the fire in your belly to move towards freedom.

Property investing is just the vehicle. Unless you have real commitment and passion to create freedom in your life, whether it's about creating more time, more money or greater legacy, you are very unlikely to achieve the results that you want.

5. Cultivate being investment agnostic

We all have biases when it comes to investing. Our biases come from how we've been educated and the experiences we've had. We can't help them.

If you strive to be investment agnostic, you don't care about which vehicle is used to get wealthy, you only care about whether the investment you are considering will make you money and whether the vehicle is a 'fit' for you.

This means that you let go of preconceived ideas of things you've heard, conversations that you may have had with other people, or education you've had in the past, that sways your opinion about the merits of a particular investment.

At the end of the day the purpose of property investing, or any investing for that matter, is that you want to be able to make money.

The beauty of cultivating an agnostic mindset is that you have no 'charge' around how you feel about different types of property investments. If you have no charge, then you are open to new opportunities.

> *The Freedom Warrior has:*
>
> *An agnostic mindset. They want to make money and are not concerned with 'right and wrong' strategies.*

While the market is in a state of flux, the more investment agnostic you are, the more the focus can be on, "How can I make money in this climate?" You might be doing things that you haven't tried before, but you're potentially increasing your probability of success in a market where most other property investors are going to be stagnant or going backward.

If you would like help with this project, go to:
http://freedomwarrior.com.au/book

Chapter 13

Elite Network

The clever pipeline owner had friends in far off places who supported him by either seeking better water sources, looking for stronger materials to use in construction, or monitoring the current pipeline performance.

Jim Rohn, a renowned motivational speaker famously once said that we are the average of the five people we spend the most time with.

Who knows if that's true.

Here is what I believe to be 100% true: your network drives your net worth.

No network, limited net worth.

Your capacity to generate relationships with good people who can support your wealth creation has the single biggest influence on your wealth position.

Knowing the right people can accelerate your journey to financial freedom, while not knowing the right people and finding opportunities on your own, is a little like trying to walk through wet cement.

Perhaps you feel like there are opportunities out there to make great returns, but you can't work out how to get access, or you feel you keep missing out. You struggle to find epic deals and recognise that your ambition and traction are a mismatch.

Maybe you don't have people in your network who can share ideas to speed up your wealth building, so you do what everyone else does; you read the occasional book when you have an ounce of energy left at the end of the night, or you scour the internet in your spare time browsing the thousands of properties online.

You may also feel many of the finance professionals you meet are not on the same page as you. Maybe they don't offer any advice other than to buy insurances, managed funds, shares or expensive properties. Or perhaps you find it hard to take someone seriously when they seem to be completely reliant on your fees as their sole source of income.

Above all else, you may be really pained by the fact that you finally have the means to do some deals, but your ability to find good opportunities is slowing you down and you are wasting valuable time.

But, here's the thing; if you find a way to build a network of people who can support your investment journey, they can bring you premium opportunities to cherry-pick from, when you tell them you are ready for your next deal.

Also, knowing people who are at the top of their game in wealth creation will immediately give you a deep well of knowledge and advice to draw from as and when you need it.

You can start to tap into a whole world of traditional and alternative property investment opportunities, which are beyond the reach of the average investor.

Finally, what you can be totally excited about is that you are on track toward creating the wealth you want. At a time when you are in your peak earning years, you can invest in opportunities that give you premium returns, because you have access to deal flow at your fingertips. You are streets ahead of other investors and have significantly more time leverage.

Three Ways To Cultivate An Elite Network:

1. Invest in Relationship Capital

I would say hands-down, my investment in key relationships has been the single biggest element of my success as an investor.

I talk about a lot of different variables that contribute to success as a property investor, but if I reflect on the last ten years of my investing journey, I think the thing that stands out as being the most critical element for success is what I would call, 'relationship capital'.

During my adult life, one of my biggest priorities has been to seek out amazing mentors and advisers - whether it's in health and fitness, spiritual & personal development, or finances and wealth.

In the space of property investing I have recognised the need to seek out people who are doing big things and can help me grow. These aren't always educators, but everyday people who are successful investors, advisers, or people with access to deal flow.

Truthfully, I tried to learn the formal way to network, but it never worked for me.

So I was surprised when I was recently interviewed for a podcast, and the interviewer commented that he thought I was one of the best networkers he'd ever met.

I am not a conscious networker. I simply like people and if I feel an affinity with people, I make an effort.

I often found going to large networking-type events very daunting, but I reconciled this eventually with the idea that I just needed to meet one person at a time. In the same way, if you're thinking about undertaking the task of building an elite network, think of it as just needing to meet one person at a time.

Think about the types of people that you need in your network in order to achieve the goals that you have around your wealth. One of the easiest places to start is to try and network with like-minded investors. That in itself will open up a whole range of other opportunities to grow your elite network through people you meet organically.

It would be my view that developing an elite network definitely does not happen overnight but requires patience and determination.

If you do very little else from this book, but you want to fast-track your results, focus on this one thing.

2. Speak to Kings

There is a common expression I've heard amongst many business people I know, which essentially says, "Kings talk to kings." The context they use this expression in is to say, if you want to get the results of the best people, then be in an environment where you can talk to them.

If you are serious about getting big results, you need to be with kings (metaphorically speaking). It will drive your ability to find good opportunities, your education, your returns and it will show you how to plan bigger, play bigger and think bigger, so that you can live bigger.

One of the most effective and powerful ways to organically educate yourself, as well as develop your network, is to join or start a mastermind. A group of like-minded people who have similar goals, want to explore ideas and opportunities together and that want to hold each other accountable.

Throughout history, there have been a number of high-profile individuals, ranging from Napoleon Hill to Anthony Robbins, who have been huge advocates for using masterminds to make better decisions and grow your network.

What's great about a network in the form of a mastermind is it gives you exposure to what lots of different people are doing, who are all thinking at the different levels to you. You get to benefit from different people's life experiences, but also benefit from the combined input from the group.

Masterminds with clear goals and philosophies also have a great capacity to harness resources that would otherwise be out of reach. Particularly in the arena of relationships, being part of a mastermind can give you access to relationships and contacts that you might otherwise never come across.

In my own mastermind, the goals are clear. There is education. There is focus. There are trusted experts who offer advice and open door to premium opportunities. There is community.

The opposite of being part of a mastermind is trying to be the do-it-yourself investor. If you have plenty of time, the capacity to educate yourself and explore opportunities, then working in isolation can be just as fruitful.

On the other hand, if you are short of time, do not have the inclination to educate yourself, are frustrated with the avalanche of information available in the marketplace, and you want to fast track your results, then a mastermind in any form will fast-track your results.

3. Make connections that grow your mind

Although it helps, developing an elite network doesn't always mean you need to be in direct communication.

If part of the purpose of developing an elite network is to raise your horizons, help you think bigger, cultivate ideas, attitudes, and habits that go beyond what you would ever hear about in your own world, you can do this from the comfort of your own home.

Watch Youtube, read articles, listen to podcasts. Find out who is revered, who is a thought leader and who might spark ideas to support your journey.

As an extension of this, find thought leaders that matter to you and find a way to connect.

If you would like help with this project, go to:
http://freedomwarrior.com.au/book

Final thoughts

Sometimes it's the small things in life that bring the greatest sense of freedom.

The freedom to spend time with our loved ones as and when we want. Not worrying about taking time off when your kids are sick, taking them to all their activities without feeling strain or being totally present when you are with them because work is no longer a distraction.

The freedom to lend a hand, or giving resources to charitable causes we believe in.

The freedom of having the money on hand to do the things that matter most to us; living where and how we want, immersing ourselves in a hobby or passion, travelling, spending money on our homes or ourselves, or the freedom to sleep in just because you feel tired.

Imagine having all this regardless of whether you turn up to work or not.

Being a freedom warrior is simply the active pursuit and protection of whatever freedom looks like to you. Property investing is still the most effective way to access the kind of financial freedom needed to cultivate a life that is filled with big and small freedoms of all flavours.

Freedom, by whatever definition is meaningful to you, is within your reach.

It's yours for the taking.

But you can't get it if you aren't fierce about it. It's not for the mild. It's for the bold.

So, are you in or out?

Here's to your freedom!

Whenever you're ready, here are 3 ways I can help you create more freedom through your property investing:

Fast Track - If you are ready to get a personalised plan and become a successful property investor, then find a time in my calendar and let's get you started. Book Now:
http://freedomwarrior.com.au/fasttrack

Nearly Ready - Jump onto our next webinar and go deeper into some basic frameworks in property investing, get some questions answered and become more familiar with the pitfalls to avoid. Register Here:
http://freedomwarrior.com.au/training

Interested but not sure - Jump into our private Facebook group and become part of our community and get some great information and insights into how to fast-track your results in property investing. Join Us:
http://freedomwarrior.com.au/fbgroup

About Salena Kulkarni

Salena Kulkarni is a Chartered Accountant and Certified Property Investment Adviser. She started her career as an accountant with Deloitte before working for a series of multinational companies all over the world.

She has been an avid property investor for two decades and became massively enthused about it as she realised the leverage it could bring to time and finances. She is passionate helping people who want to use their hard-earned income to create the most amplified wealth they can via property.

She now works as a property strategist and mentor to help people fast-track their success with property investing with attention to their unique situation, risk profile, goals and means.

Her latest program Freedom Warrior™ is a Mastermind for business owners and executives who want to fast-track their results in property investing. She shares a whole new world of property investing strategies, unique education and frameworks and shares her high-end network.

For more information go to: http://freedomwarrior.com.au/mastermind

Notes

Notes

Notes

Notes

Notes

Notes

Notes

Notes

Notes

Notes

Notes

Made in United States
North Haven, CT
30 March 2022